Family Knits

Over 25 knitwear designs for babies, children and adults

Debbie Bliss

Trafalgar Square Publishing

This book is dedicated to the life of Stephen Kemp

First published in the United States of America in 1998 by
Trafalgar Square Publishing, North Pomfret, Vermont 05053

Printed and bound in Singapore by Tien Wah Press

ISBN 1-57076-123-X

Library of Congress Catalog Card Number: 98-84288

Photography by Pia Tryde
Design by Alison Shackleton
Styling by Karen McCartney and Alyson Walsh
Pattern checking by Tina Egleton

CONTENTS

Introduction

The Family Collection has been a wonderful opportunity for me to include, for the first time, a range of handknit designs for adults as well as children.

There are 21 styles to choose from – delicate florals in soft antique shades, denim knits inspired by fisherman sweaters, sporty knits with a stars and hearts theme and cabled classics in soft tweeds. Most range in size from toddler up to adult and some have variations such as jacket style or an alternative collar.

I hope there will be designs here for everyone to enjoy. With this in mind I have included styles to suit all shapes, from the neatly tailored to the more generous tunics. The patterns are also designed to suit knitters of all levels of skill with both easy and advanced knits, stitch textures and colour patterning.

Basic information

Notes

Figures for larger sizes are given in round ( ) brackets. Where only one figure appears, this applies to all sizes. Work figures given in square [ ] brackets the number of times stated afterwards. Alternatively, figures in square brackets give the resultant number of stitches.

Where 0 appears, no stitches or rows are worked for this size.

The yarn amounts given in the instructions are based on average requirements and should therefore be considered approximate. If you want to use a substitute yarn, choose a yarn of the same type and weight as the one recommended. The following descriptions of the various Rowan yarns are meant as a guide to the yarn weight and type (i.e., cotton, mohair, wool, etc.). Remember that the description of the yarn weight is only a rough guide and you should always test a yarn first to see if it will achieve the correct tension.

Magpie Aran: a fisherman medium-weight yarn (100% pure new wool); approximately 150m/164yd per 100g/3½oz hank.

Cotton Glacé: a lightweight cotton yarn (100% cotton); approximately 112m/123yd per 50g/1¾oz ball.

Designer DK: a double knitting-weight yarn (100% pure new wool); approximately 115m/125yd per 50g/1¾oz ball.

Handknit DK Cotton: a medium-weight cotton yarn (100% cotton); approximately 85m/90yd per 50g/1¾oz ball.

True 4-ply Botany: a 4-ply yarn (100% pure new wool; approximately 170m/220yd per 50g/1¾oz ball.

DK Tweed: a double knitting-weight yarn (100% pure new wool); approximately 110m/120yd per 50g/1¾ oz ball.

Chunky: a chunky weight yarn (100% wool); approximately 120m/130yd per 100g/3¾oz hank.

Chunky Chenille: a chunky weight chenille yarn (100% cotton);

approximately 140m/153yd per 100g/3¾ oz ball.

The amount of a substitute yarn needed is determined by the number of metres/yards needed rather than by the number of grams/ounces. If you are unsure when choosing a substitute, ask your yarn shop to advise you.

Tension

Each pattern in this book specifies a tension – the number of stitches and rows per centimetre/inch that should be obtained with the given needles, yarn and stitch pattern. Check your tension carefully before commencing work.

Use the same yarn, needles and stitch pattern as those to be used for the main work and knit a sample at least 12.5cm/5in square. Smooth out the finished sample on a flat surface, but do not stretch it. To check the tension, place a ruler horizontally on the sample and mark 10cm/4in across with pins. Count the number of stitches between the pins. To check the row tension, place a ruler vertically on the sample and mark 10cm/4in with pins. Count the number of rows between the pins. If the number of stitches and rows is greater than specified, try again using larger needles; if less, use smaller needles.

The stitch tension is the most important element to get right.

In the US, balls or hanks of yarn are sold in ounces, not in grams; the weights of the relevant Rowan yarns are given opposite. In addition, a few specific knitting or crochet terms may be unfamiliar to some readers. The list below explains the abbreviations used in this book to help the reader understand how to follow the various stitches and stages.

Standard abbreviations

alt = alternate
beg = begin(ning)
cont = continue
dec = decreas(e)ing
foll = following
inc = increas(e)ing
k = knit
m1 = make one by picking up the loop lying just between st just worked and next st and working into the back of it
patt = pattern
p = purl
psso = pass slipped stitch over
rem = remaining
rep = repeat
skpo = slip 1, knit 1, pass slipped stitch over
sl = slip
st(s) = stitch(es)
st st = stocking stitch
tbl = through back of loop
tog = together
yb = yarn back
yf = yarn forward
yon = yarn over needle
yrn = yarn round needle

The following terms may be unfamiliar to US readers;

UK terms	US terms
Aran wool	'fisherman' (unbleached wool) yarn
ball band	yarn wrapper
cast off	bind off
DK wool	knitting worsted yarn
double crochet stitch	single crochet stitch
make up (garment)	finish (garment)
rib	ribbing
stocking stitch	stockinette stitch
tension	gauge

Important

Check on ball band for washing instructions. After washing, pat garments into shape and dry flat, away from direct heat.

Rowan Denim will shrink and fade when it is washed, just like a pair of jeans. Unlike many 'denim look' yarns, this one uses real indigo dye which only coats the surface of the yarn, leaving a white core that is gradually exposed through washing and wearing.

When washed for the first time, the yarn will shrink by up to one-fifth on length; the width, however, will remain the same. all the necessary adjustments have been made in the instructions for the patterns specially designed for Denim.

The knitted pieces should be washed separately at a temperature of 60–70°C (140–158°F) before you sew the garment together. The pieces can then be tumble-dried. Dye loss will be greatest during the initial wash; the appearance of the garment will, however, be greatly enhanced with additional washing and wearing. The cream denim yarn will shrink in the same way but will not fade.

ARAN LACE-EDGED CARDIGAN

This boxy cardigan with cable and lace panels has a pretty, easy to knit lace edging. The design shown is a cropped style, but it can easily be lengthened if you prefer a longer look.

MATERIALS
14(15:16) 50g balls of Rowan Cotton Glace.
Pair each of 2¾mm (No 12/US 2) and 3¼mm (No 10/US 3) knitting needles.
Cable needle.
4 buttons.

TENSION
25 sts and 34 rows to 10cm/4in square over st st on 3¼mm (No 10/US 3) needles.
23 sts of panel A pattern measures 7cm/2¾in on 3¼mm (No 10/US 3) needles.

ABBREVIATIONS
C4F = sl next 2 sts onto cable needle and leave at front of work, k2, then k2 from cable needle;
Cr3L = sl next 2 sts onto cable needle and leave at front of work, p1, then k2 from cable needle;
Cr3R = sl next st onto cable needle and leave at back of work, k2, then p1 from cable needle;
Tw4L = sl next 3 sts onto cable needle and leave at front of work, k1, then k1 tbl, p1, k1 tbl from cable needle;
Tw4R = sl next st onto cable needle and leave at back of work, k1 tbl, p1, k1 tbl, then k st from cable needle;
mb = [k1, yf, k1, yf, k1] all in next st, turn, p5, turn, k3, k2 tog, then pass 2nd, 3rd and 4th st over 1st st.
Also see page 7.

MEASUREMENTS

To fit bust	86	91	97 cm
	34	36	38 in
Actual bust measurement	98	103	108 cm
	38½	40½	42½ in
Length	42	45	48 cm
	16½	17¾	19 in
Sleeve seam	44	45	46 cm
	17¼	17¾	18 in

PANEL A
Worked over 23 sts.
1st row (wrong side) K8, p1, k1, p3, k1, p1, k8.
2nd row P7, Tw4R, k1 tbl, Tw4L, p7.
3rd row K7, p1, [k1, p1] 4 times, k7.
4th row P6, Tw4R, k1, k1 tbl, k1, Tw4L, p6.
5th row K6, p1, k1, p1, [k2, p1] twice, k1, p1, k6.
6th row P5, Tw4R, k2, k1 tbl, k2, Tw4L, p5.
7th row K5, p1, k1, p2, k2, p1, k2, p2, k1, p1, k5.
8th row P4, Tw4R, k1 tbl, [k2, k1 tbl] twice, Tw4L, p4.
9th row K4, p1, [k1, p1] twice, [k2, p1] twice, [k1, p1] twice, k4.
10th row P3, Tw4R, k1, k1 tbl, [k2, k1 tbl] twice, k1, Tw4L, p3.
11th row K3, p1, k1, p1, [k2, p1] 4 times, k1, p1, k3.
12th row P2, Tw4R, k2, [k1 tbl, k2] 3 times, Tw4L, p2.
13th row K2, p1, k1, p1, k3, p1, [k2, p1] twice, k3, p1, k1, p1, k2.
14th row P2, k1 tbl, p1, k1 tbl, k3, mb, [k2, mb] twice, k3, k1 tbl, p1, k1 tbl, p2.
15th row K2, p1, k1, p1, k3, p1 tbl, [k2, p1 tbl] twice, k3, p1, k1, p1, k2.
16th row P2, k1 tbl, p1, k1 tbl, p3, k1 tbl, p1, k3 tbl, p1, k1 tbl, p3, k1 tbl, p1, k1 tbl, p2.
These 16 rows form patt.

PANEL B
Worked over 8 sts.
1st row (wrong side) K1, p2, k5.
2nd row P2, mb, p1, Cr3R, p1.
3rd row K2, p2, k4.
4th row P3, Cr3R, p2.
5th row K3, p2, k3.
6th row P2, Cr3R, p3.
7th row K4, p2, k2.
8th row P1, Cr3R, p4.
9th row K5, p2, k1.
10th row P1, Cr3L, p1, mb, p2.
11th row K4, p2, k2.
12th row P2, Cr3L, p3.
13th row K3, p2, k3.
14th row P3, Cr3L, p2.
15th row K2, p2, k4.
16th row P4, Cr3L, p1.
These 16 rows form patt.

BACK
With 3¼mm (No 10/US 3) needles cast on 160(166:172) sts.
1st row (wrong side) K4(7:10), [work 1st row of panel A, p4, work 9th row of panel B, p4] twice, work 1st row of panel B, p4, work 1st row of panel A, p4, work 1st row of panel B, p4, work 1st row of panel A, k4(7:10).
2nd row K4(7:10), work 2nd row of panel A, C4F, work 2nd row of panel B, C4F, work 2nd row of panel A, C4F, work 2nd row of panel B, [C4F, work

10th row of panel B, C4F, work 2nd row of panel A] twice, k4(7:10).
3rd row K4(7:10), [work 3rd row of panel A, p4, work 11th row of panel B, p4] twice, work 3rd row of panel B, p4, work 3rd row of panel A, p4, work 3rd row of panel B, p4, work 3rd row of panel A, k4(7:10).
4th row K4(7:10), [work 4th row of panel A, k4, work 4th row of panel B, k4] twice, work 12th row of panel B, k4, work 4th row of panel A, k4, work 12th row of panel B, k4, work 4th row of panel A, k4(7:10).
These 4 rows set position of panels, form cable patt between panels and garter st at side edges. Cont in patt until work measures 40(43:46)cm/15¾ (17:18¼)in from beg, ending with a wrong side row.
Shape Shoulders
Cast off 29(30:31) sts at beg of next 2 rows and 30(31:32) sts at beg of foll 2 rows. Cast off rem 42(44:46) sts.

LEFT FRONT
With 3¼mm (No 10/US 3) needles cast on 84(87:90) sts.
1st row (wrong side) K6, work 1st row of panel B, p4, work 1st row of panel A, p4, work 1st row of panel B, p4, work 1st row of panel A, k4(7:10).
2nd row K4(7:10), work 2nd row of panel A, C4F, work 2nd row of panel B, C4F, work 2nd row of panel A, C4F, work 2nd row of panel B, k6.
3rd row K6, work 3rd row of panel B, p4, work 3rd row of panel A, p4, work 3rd row of panel B, p4, work 3rd row of panel A, k4(7:10).
4th row K4(7:10), work 4th row of panel A, k4, work 4th row of panel B, k4, work 4th row of panel A, k4, work 4th row of panel B, k6.
These 4 rows set position of panels, form cable patt between panels and garter st at side edges. Cont in patt until work measures 23(25:27)cm/9 (10:10¾)in from beg, ending with a right side row.

Shape Neck
Keeping patt correct, cast off 6 sts at beg of next row. Dec one st at neck edge on every right side row until 59(61:63) sts rem. Cont straight until Front matches Back to shoulder shaping, ending with a wrong side row.
Shape Shoulder
Cast off 29(30:31) sts at beg of next row. Work 1 row. Cast off rem 30(31:32) sts.
Mark front edge to indicate buttons: first one 3 rows up from lower edge, last one 4 rows below neck shaping and rem 2 evenly spaced between.

RIGHT FRONT
With 3¼mm (No 10/US 3) needles cast on 84(87:90) sts.
1st row (wrong side) K4(7:10), work 1st row of panel A, p4, work 9th row of panel B, p4, work 1st row of panel A, p4, work 9th row of panel B, k6.
2nd row K6, work 10th row of panel B, C4F, work 2nd row of panel A, C4F, work 10th row of panel B, C4F, work 2nd row of panel A, k4(7:10).
3rd row K4(7:10), work 3rd row of panel A, p4, work 11th row of panel B, p4, work 3rd row of panel A, p4, work 11th row of panel B, k6.
4th (buttonhole) row K1, k2 tog, yf, k3, work 12th row of panel B, k4, work 4th row of panel A, k4, work 12th row of panel B, k4, work 4th row of panel A, k4(7:10).
These 4 rows set position of panels, form cable patt between panels and garter st at side edges. Complete as given for Left Front, reversing shapings and making buttonholes as before to match markers.

SLEEVES
With 3¼mm (No 10/US 3) needles cast on 84(86:88) sts.
1st row (wrong side) K1(2:3), p4, work 1st row of panel A, p4, work 9th row of panel B, p4, work 1st row of panel B, p4, work 1st row of panel A, p4, k1(2:3).
2nd row K0(1:2), p1, C4F, work 2nd row of panel A, C4F, work 2nd row of panel B, C4F, work 10th row of panel B, C4F, work 2nd row of panel A, C4F, p1, k0(1:2).
3rd row K1(2:3), p4, work 3rd row of panel A, p4, work 11th row of panel B, p4, work 3rd row of panel B, p4, work 3rd row of panel A, p4, k1(2:3).
4th row K0(1:2), p1, k4 work 4th row of panel A, k4, work 4th row of panel B, k4, work 12th row of panel B, k4, work 4th row of panel A, k4, p1, k0(1:2).
These 4 rows set position of panels and form cable patt between panels. Cont in patt, inc one st at each end of 5th row and 1(6:8) foll 4th rows then on every foll 6th row until there are 124(130:136) sts, working inc sts into garter st. Cont straight until work measures 42(43:44)cm/16½(17:17¼)in from beg, ending with a wrong side row. Cast off.

WELT EDGING
With 2¾mm (No 12/US 2) needles cast on 4 sts. K 1 row.
1st row (wrong side) K2, yf, k2.
2nd row and 2 foll alt rows Sl 1, k to end.
3rd row K3, yf, k2.
5th row K2, yf, k2 tog, yf, k2.
7th row K3, yf, k2 tog, yf, k2.
8th row Cast off 4, k to end.
These 8 rows form patt. Cont in patt until edging, when slightly stretched, fits along lower edge of back and both fronts, ending with 8th patt row. Cast off.

SLEEVE EDGINGS (MAKE 2)
Work as given for Welt Edging until edging, when slightly stretched, fits along lower edge of sleeve, ending with 8th patt row. Cast off.

COLLAR
Join shoulder seams.
Work as given for Welt Edging, inc one st at beg of 3rd patt row and 12 foll

4th rows, working inc sts as k. Cont straight until collar, when slightly stretched, fits shaped edge of Right Front to centre of back neck, ending with 8th patt row. Work other half of collar to match, working dec instead of inc and ending with 8th patt row. Cast off.

TO MAKE UP

Sew sleeve edgings in place. Sew on sleeves, placing centre of sleeves to shoulder seams. Join side and sleeve seams. Sew on welt edging and collar in place, beginning and ending at centre of front bands. Sew on buttons.

Aran Lace-edged Cardigan (left) and Guernsey with Bobble Edging (right; see page 12)

GUERNSEY WITH BOBBLE EDGING

Worked in classic cables and moss stitch diamonds, this guernsey-inspired design has a triangular garter stitch border with bobbles. If you prefer a less decorative collar, you can work the plain neckband instead (see detail overleaf).

MATERIALS

8(9:12:14:18:20:21) 50g balls of Rowan Cotton Glace.
Pair of 3¼mm (No 10/US 3) knitting needles.
Cable needle.

MEASUREMENTS

To fit ages/sizes	1-2yrs	3-5yrs	6-9yrs	10-12 yrs	small	medium	large
Actual chest/bust measurement	70	82	100	112	112	128	140 cm
	27½	32¼	39½	44	44	50½	55 in
Length	40	46	52	60	70	74	78 cm
	15¾	18¼	20½	23¾	27½	29¼	30¾ in
Sleeve seam	22	28	34	40	44	46	48 cm
	8¾	11	13½	15¾	17¼	18	19 in

TENSION

25 sts and 34 rows to 10cm/4in square over st st on 3¼mm (No 10/US 3) needles.
14 sts of panel B pattern measures 4cm/1½in, 24 sts of panel D pattern measures 6cm/2¼in on 3¼mm (No 10/US 3) needles.

ABBREVIATIONS

C3B = sl next st onto cable needle and leave at back of work, k2, then k st from cable needle;
C3F = sl next 2 sts onto cable needle and leave at front of work, k1, then k2 from cable needle;
C4B = sl next 2 sts onto cable needle and leave at back of work, k2, then k2 from cable needle;
C4F = sl next 2 sts onto cable needle and leave at front of work, k2, then k2 from cable needle;
C5B = sl next 2 sts onto cable needle and leave at back of work, k3, then k2 from cable needle;
C5F = sl next 3 sts onto cable needle and leave at front of work, k2, then k3 from cable needle;
C6B = sl next 3 sts onto cable needle and leave at back of work, k3, then k3 from cable needle;
Cr3L = sl next 2 sts onto cable needle and leave at front of work, p1, then k2 from cable needle;
Cr3R = sl next st onto cable needle and leave at back of work, k2, then p st from cable needle;
Cr4L = sl next 2 sts onto cable needle and leave at front of work, p2, then k2 from cable needle;
Cr4R = sl next 2 sts onto cable needle and leave at back of work, k2, then p2 from cable needle;
Cr5L = sl next 3 sts onto cable needle and leave at front of work, p2, then k3 from cable needle;
Cr5R = sl next 2 sts onto cable needle and leave at back of work, k3, then p2 from cable needle.
Also see page 7.

PANEL A

Worked over 7 sts.
1st row (right side) P3, p into front, back, front, back, front, back of next st, then pass 2nd, 3rd, 4th, 5th and 6th sts over 1st st, p3.
2nd, 3rd, 4th, 5th and 6th rows P7.
These 6 rows form patt.

PANEL B

Worked over 14 sts.
1st row (right side) P3, k8, p3.
2nd row K3, p8, k3.
3rd row P4, C3B, Cr3L, p4.
4th row K4, p3, k1, p2, k4.
5th row P3, Cr3R, k1, p1, C3F, p3.
6th row K3, p2, k1, p1, k1, p3, k3.
7th row P2, C3B, [p1, k1] twice, Cr3L, p2.
8th row K2, p3, k1, [p1, k1] twice, p2, k2.
9th row P1, Cr3R, [k1, p1] 3 times, C3F, p1.
10th row K1, p2, k1, [p1, k1] 3 times, p3, k1.
11th row P1, Cr3L, [k1, p1] 3 times, Cr3R, p1.
12th row As 8th row.
13th row P2, Cr3L, [p1, k1] twice, Cr3R, p2.
14th row As 6th row.
15th row P3, Cr3L, k1, p1, Cr3R, p3.
16th row As 4th row.
17th row P4, Cr3L, Cr3R, p4.
18th row K5, p4, k5.
19th row P3, C4B, C4F, p3.
20th row K3, p8, k3.
21st and 22nd rows As 1st and 2nd rows.
23rd and 24th rows As 19th and 20th rows.
These 24 rows form patt.

PANEL C

Worked over 11 sts.
1st row (right side) K11.

2nd row P11.
3rd row K5, p1, k5.
4th row P4, k1, p1, k1, p4.
5th row K3, p1, [k1, p1] twice, k3.
6th row P2, k1, [p1, k1] 3 times, p2.
7th row K1, [p1, k1] 5 times.
8th row As 6th row.
9th row As 5th row.
10th row As 4th row.
11th row As 3rd row.
12th row P11.
13th row K11.
14th row P11.
These 14 rows form patt.

PANEL D
Worked over 24 sts.
1st row (right side) P1, k2, p6, C6B, p6, k2, p1.
2nd row K1, p22, k1.
3rd row P1, k2, p4, Cr5R, Cr5L, p4, k2, p1.
4th row K1, p9, k4, p9, k1.
5th row P1, Cr4L, Cr5R, p4, Cr5L, Cr4R, p1.
6th row K3, p5, k8, p5, k3.
7th row P3, C5B, p4, mb thus: pick up loop lying between st just worked and next st and work into front, back, front, back and front of the loop, then pass 2nd, 3rd, 4th and 5th sts over 1st st, p1, then pass bobble st over the p st just worked, p3, C5F, p3.
8th row As 6th row.
9th row P1, Cr5R, Cr4L, p4, Cr4R, Cr5L, p1.
10th row As 4th row.
11th row P1, k3, [p4, k2] twice, p4, k3, p1.
12th row As 4th row.
13th row P1, k3, p4, k2, p2, mb (as in 7th row), p1, pass bobble st over the p st just worked, p1, k2, p4, k3, p1.
14th to 16th rows Work 10th to 12th rows.
17th row P1, Cr5L, Cr4R, p4, Cr4L, Cr5R, p1.
18th row As 6th row.
19th row P3, C5F, p4, mb (as in 7th row), p1, pass bobble st over the p st just worked, p3, C5B, p3.
20th row As 6th row.
21st row P1, Cr4R, Cr5L, p4, Cr5R, Cr4L, p1.
22nd row As 4th row.
23rd row P1, k2, p4, Cr5L, Cr5R, p4, k2, p1.
24th row As 2nd row.
These 24 rows form patt.

BACK
With 3¼mm (No 10/US 3) needles cast on 102(116:138:152:152:180:194) sts.
Beg with a k row, work 4(6:8:10:14:15:16)cm/1½(2¼:3:4:5½:6:6¼)in in st st, ending with a p row.
1st size
1st row (right side) Work 1st row of panels B, A, C, A, D, A, C, A and B.
2nd size
1st row (right side) Work 1st row of panels A, B, A, C, A, D, A, C, A, B and A.
3rd size
1st row (right side) Work 1st row of panels C, A, B, A, C, A, D, A, C, A, B, A and C.
4th and 5th sizes
1st row (right side) Work 1st row of

panels A, C, A, B, A, C, A, D, A, C, A, B, A, C and A.

6th size

1st row (right side) Work 1st row of panels [B, A, C, A] twice, D, [A, C, A, B] twice.

7th size

1st row (right side) Work 1st row of panels [A, B, A, C] twice, A, D, A, [C, A, B, A] twice.

All sizes

The last row sets position of panels. ** Cont in patt until work measures 37(43:49:57:67:71:75)cm/14½(17:19¼:22½:26¼:28:29½)in from beg, ending with a wrong side row.

Shape Shoulders

Cast off 16(19:24:27:27:33:36) sts at beg of next 2 rows and 17(20:24:27:27:33:36) sts at beg of foll 2 rows. Leave rem 36(38:42:44:44:48:50) sts on a holder.

Welt

With 3¼mm (No 10/US 3) needles and right side facing, k up 90(99:126:135:135:162:171) sts along lower edge of Back. K 5 rows.

* **Next row** K9, turn.

Work on these 9 sts only.

Next row K2 tog, k2, k into front, back, front, back, front and back of next st, then pass 2nd, 3rd, 4th, 5th and 6th sts over 1st st – leave bobble on right side of work, k2, k2 tog tbl.

K 1 row.

Next row K2 tog, k3, k2 tog tbl.

K 1 row.

Next row K2 tog, k1, k2 tog tbl.

K 1 row. K3 tog and fasten off. Rejoin yarn at inside edge to rem sts and work from * until all sts are worked off.

FRONT

Work as given for Back to **. Cont in patt until work measures 33(38:44:52:61:65:69)cm/13(15:17¼:20½:24:25½:27¼)in from beg, ending with a wrong side row.

Shape Neck

Next row Patt 41(48:57:63:63:76:82), turn.

Work on this set of sts only. Dec one st at neck edge on every row until 33(39:48:54:54:66:72) sts rem. Cont straight until Front matches Back to shoulder shaping, ending at side edge.

Shape Shoulder

Cast off 16(19:24:27:27:33:36) sts at beg of next row. Work 1 row. Cast off rem 17(20:24:27:27:33:36) sts.

With right side facing, slip centre 20(20:24:26:26:28:30) sts onto a holder, rejoin yarn and patt to end. Complete as given for first side.

Welt

Work as given for Back Welt.

SLEEVES

With 3¼mm (No 10/US 3) needles cast on 50(50:60:60:60:66:66) sts.

1st and 2nd sizes

1st row (right side) K6 – last 6 sts of panel C, work 1st row of panels A, D and A, k6 – first 6 sts of panel C.

3rd, 4th and 5th sizes

1st row (right side) Work 1st row of panels C, A, D, A and C.

6th and 7th sizes

1st row (right side) P3 – last 3 sts of panel A, work 1st row of panels C, A, D, A and C, p3 - first 3 sts of panel A.

All sizes

The last row sets position of panels. Cont in patt, inc one st at each end of 7th row and every foll 5th(6th:6th:5th:5th:4th:4th) row until there are 72(76:90:102:116:128:138) sts, working inc sts into patt to match Back. Cont straight until Sleeve measures 19(25:31:37:41:43:45)cm/7½(9¾:12¼:14½:16:16¾:17¾)in from beg, ending with a wrong side row. Cast off.

Cuffs

With 3¼mm (No 10/US 3) needles and right side facing, k up 45(45:54:54:54:63:63) sts along lower edge of sleeve. Complete as given for Back Welt.

COLLAR

Join right shoulder seam. With 3¼mm (No 10/US 3) needles and right side facing, k up 19(22:22:22:25:25:25) sts down left front neck, k centre front sts dec 4 sts evenly, k up 18(21:21:21:24:24:24) sts up right front neck, k back neck sts dec 4 sts evenly. 85(93:101:105:111:117:121) sts.

1st row K1, [p1, k1] to end.

2nd row P1, [k1, p1] to end.

Rep last 2 rows 3(3:4:4:5:5:5) times more. Rib 1 row, dec 4(3:2:6:3:0:4) sts evenly across last row. 81(90:99:99:108:117:117) sts. K 5(5:7:7:9:9:9) rows. Work as given for Back Welt from * to end. K14(14:18:18:22:22:22). Cast off.

NECKBAND

Join right shoulder seam. With 3¼mm (No.10/US3) needles and right side facing, k up 16(19:19:19:22:22:22) sts down left front neck, k centre front sts dec 4 sts evenly, k up 15(18:18:18:21:21:21) sts up right front neck, k back neck sts dec 6 sts evenly. 77(85:93:97:103:109:113) sts. K5(5:5:5:7:7:7) rows. Cast off.

TO MAKE UP

Join left shoulder and collar or neckband seam, reversing seam on garter stitch edge of collar. Sew on sleeves, placing centre of sleeves to shoulder seams. Join side and sleeve seams.

TRADITIONAL GUERNSEY

This sweater is based on a classic fisherman's guernsey and has a ribbed yoke. It is worked using the traditional method on a circular needle, with shoulder and armhole gussets. The sleeves are knitted from the shoulders down to the wrist.

MATERIALS
5(5:6:6:7:8:9:10:11:12:13) 50g balls of Rowan True 4 ply Botany.
Pair each of 2¾mm (No 12/US 2) and 3¼mm (No 10/US 3) knitting needles.
One 3¼mm (No 10/US 3) circular needle 40(40:50:50:50:60:60:70:70:80:80)cm/16(16:20:20:20:24:24:28:28:32:32)in long.
Set of four in each of 2¾mm (No 12/US 2) and 3¼mm (No 10/US 3) open ended knitting needles.

TENSION
28 sts and 36 rows to 10cm/4in square over st st on 3¼mm (No 10/US 3) needles.

ABBREVIATIONS
See page 7.

MEASUREMENTS

To fit ages	2yrs	3-4yrs	4-5yrs	5-6yrs	7-8yrs	8-9yrs	9-10yrs	
Actual chest/bust measurement	60	66	71	77	82	88	94	cm
	23½	26	28	30¼	32¼	34½	37	in
Length	35	39	43	47	51	55	59	cm
	13¾	15½	17	18½	20	21½	23¼	in
Sleeve seam	21	24	27	30	33	37	40	cm
	8¼	9½	10½	11¾	13	14½	15¾	in

To fit adult sizes	small	medium	large	extra large	
Actual chest/bust measurement	100	106	111	117	cm
	39½	41¾	43¾	46	in
Length	63	65	67	69	cm
	24¾	25½	26¼	27	in
Sleeve seam	43	45	47	49	cm
	17	17¾	18½	19¼	in

BACK AND FRONT
Worked in one piece to armholes.
With 2¾mm (No 12/US 2) needles, cast on 84(92:100:108:116:124:132:140:148:156:164) sts for back welt. K 13(13:13:13:15:15:15:17:17:17:17) rows. Leave these sts on a spare needle.
Work front welt in same way.
Change to 3¼mm (No 10/US 3) circular needle.
Next round K front welt sts, then k back welt sts. 168(184:200:216:232:248:264:280:296:312:328) sts. Mark end of last round to denote end of rounds.
1st round *P1, k82(90:98:106:114:122:130:138:146:154:162), p1; rep from * once more.
2nd round K.
Rep last 2 rounds until work measures 16(18:20:22:24:26:28:30:31:32:33)cm/6½(7¼:8:8¾:9½:10¼:11:11¾:12¼:12½:13)in from beg, ending with a 2nd round.
Inc round [P1, k1, m1, k1, p1] to end. 210(230:250:270:290:310:330:350:370:390:410) sts.
Work in rib patt as follows:
1st round *K4, p2, [k3, p2] 19(21:23:25:27:29:31:33:35:37:39) times, k4; rep from * once more.
2nd round [P1, k3, p1] to end.
These 2 rounds form rib. Cont in rib until work measures 20(22:24:26:29:31:34:36:37:38:39)cm/8(8¾:9½:10¼:11½:12¼:13½:14:14½:15:15½)in from beg, ending with a 1st round.
Shape Underarm Gussets
Next round *P1, m1, rib 103(113:123:133:143:153:163:173:183:193:203), m1, p1; rep from * once more.
Working inc sts as k, work 3 rounds straight.
Next round *P1, k1, m1, rib 103(113:123:133:143:153:163:173:183:193:203), m1, k1, p1; rep from * once more.
Work 3 rounds straight.
Next round *P1, k2, m1, rib 103(113:123:133:143:153:163:173:183:193:203), m1, k2, p1; rep from * once more.
Cont in this way, inc 2 sts as set at each side on 3(3:3:3:3:3:3:4:4:4:4) foll 4th rounds. Work 1 round straight. Break off yarn.
Divide for Back
Next row Sl last 7(7:7:7:7:7:7:8:8:8:8) sts of last round and next 7(7:7:7:7:7:7:8:8:8:8) sts onto a holder, rejoin yarn to rem sts, m1 (for selvedge), rib 103(113:123:133:143:153:163:173:183:193:203), m1 (for selvedge), turn.
Work on this set of sts only.

Next row (wrong side) P4, k2, [p3, k2] to last 4 sts, p4.
Next row K4, p2, [k3, p2] to last 4 sts, k4.
Rep last 2 rows until work measures 35(39:43:47:51:55:59:63:65:67:69)cm/ 13¾(15½:17:18½:20:21½:23¼:24¾:25½:26¼:27)in from beg, ending with a wrong side row.
Dec row K2, k2 tog, p2, [k1, k2 tog, p2] to last 4 sts, k1, k2 tog, k1. 84(92: 100:108:116:124:132:140:148:156:164) sts.
Leave these sts on a spare needle.
With right side facing, return to sts rem on needle for front, sl first 14(14:14:14: 14:14:14:16:16:16:16) sts onto a holder, rejoin yarn, m1, rib to end, m1, turn.
Complete as given for Back.

Shape Shoulders and Neck Gusset

With 3¼mm (No 10/US 3) needles, wrong sides of back and front together and beg at outside edge, cast off together (see diagrams) 21(23:27:29:31: 35:37:37:41:43:47) sts from each needle, leave last st on right hand needle, k next st, turn.
Next row Sl 1, p2, turn.
Next row Sl 1, k3, turn.
Next row Sl 1, p4, turn.
Next row Sl 1, k5, turn.
Cont in this way until there are 18(20:20:20:22:22:22:24:24:24:24) sts for gusset, turn.
Next row Sl 1, p8(9:9:9:10:10:10:11: 11:11:11), m1, p10(11:11:11:12:12:12: 13:13:13:13), turn.
Leave these sts.
Work other shoulder in same way.

Neckband

With set of four 2¾mm (No 12/US 2) needles and right side facing, rib as set the 88(96:96:104:112:112:120:136: 136:144:144) sts around neck. Rib a further 7(7:9:9:11:11:13:13:15:15:15) rounds. P 2 rounds. K 2 rounds. Cast off knitwise.

SLEEVES

With set of four 3¼mm (No 10/US 3) needles and right side facing, sl first 7(7:7:7:7:7:7:8:8:8:8) sts from underarm gusset onto one needle, join in yarn and with next needle, p1, k6(6:6:6:6:6: 6:7:7:7:7) rem sts, k up 73(83:93:103: 113:123:133:143:143:153:163) sts around armhole edge arranging needles as required, k6(6:6:6:6:6:6:7:7:7:7), p1 sts of gusset.
87(97:107:117:127:137:147:159:159: 169:179) sts.
1st round K10(10:10:10:10:10:10:11: 11:11:11), [p2, k3] 13(15:17:19:21:23:25: 27:27:29:31) times, p2, k10(10:10:10:10: 10:10:11:11:11:11).
2nd round P1, k5(5:5:5:5:5:5:6:6:6:6), k2 tog, k2, [p2, k3] 13(15:17:19:21:23: 25:27:27:29:31) times, p2, k2, skpo, k5(5:5:5:5:5:5:6:6:6:6), p1.
These 2 rounds set rib patt. Work 3 rounds straight.
Next round P1, k4(4:4:4:4:4:4:5:5:5:5), k2 tog, rib 71(81:91:101:111:121:131: 141:141:151:161) sts, skpo, k4(4:4:4:4: 4:5:5:5:5), p1.
Work 3 rounds straight.
Next round P1, k3(3:3:3:3:3:3:4:4:4:4), k2 tog, rib 71(81:91:101:111:121:131: 141:141:151:161), skpo, k3(3:3:3:3: 3:4:4:4:4), p1.
Cont in this way, dec 2 sts as set on 3(3:3:3:3:3:3:4:4:4:4) foll 4th rounds. 75(85:95:105:115:125:135:145:145:155: 165) sts. Cont in rib until work measures 7(8:9:10:11:11:12:13:15: 16:17)cm/2¾(3:3½:4:4¼:4¼:4¾:5¼:6:6¼: 6¾)in from beg, ending with a 1st round.
Next round P1, k1, k2 tog, [p2, k1, k2 tog] 14(16:18:20:22:24:26:28:28:30:32) times, p1. 60(68:76:84:92:100:108: 116:116:124:132) sts.
Keeping the 2 sts at seam as before and remainder in st st (every round k), work 7(3:1:3:3:1:1:1:1:3:5) rounds.
Dec round P1, k2 tog, k to last 3 sts, skpo, p1.
Work 5(5:5:3:3:3:3:3:3:3:3) rounds straight. Rep last 6(6:6:4:4:4:4:4:4:4:4) rounds until 52(56:60:60:64:64:68:72: 72:80:88) sts rem. Work 4(2:0:2:2:2:2:0:0:2:4) rounds straight.
Change to set of four 2¾mm (No 12/US 2) needles.
Next round [P1, k2, p1] to end.
Rep last round until welt measures 6cm/2½in. Cast off in rib.

A

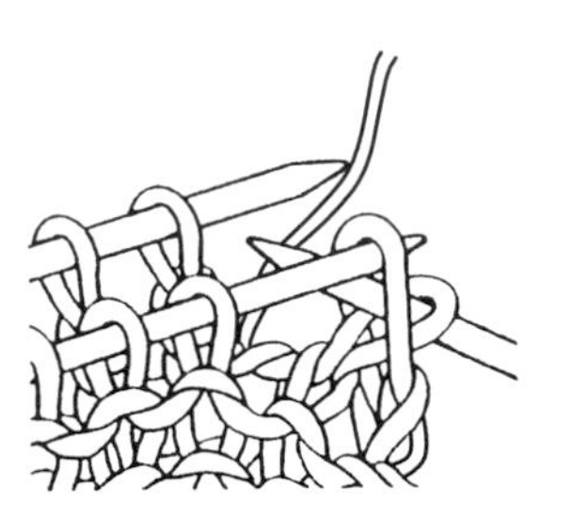

B

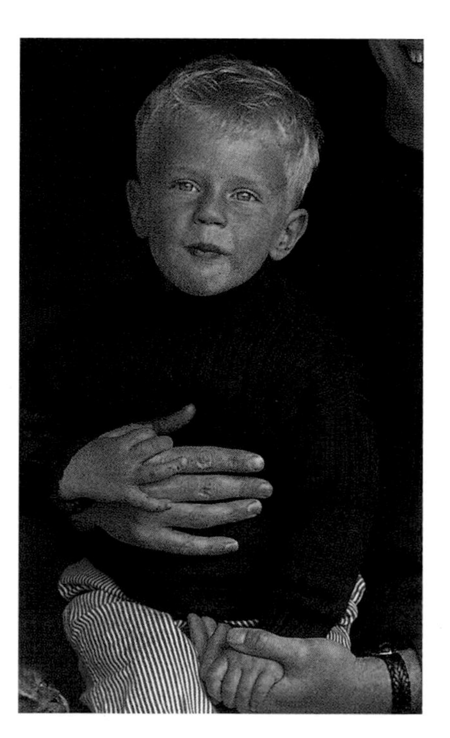

Fairisle sweater

This is a very simple fairisle to work and would be particularly suitable for a knitter who is just beginning to tackle colour. It has a neat, boxy shape and moss stitch borders.

MEASUREMENTS

To fit ages	2-3yrs	3-5yrs	5-7yrs	7-9yrs	9-11yrs	
Actual chest/bust	79	86	93	100	107	cm
measurement	31	34	36½	39½	42	in
Length	37	42	46	52	56	cm
	14½	16½	18	20½	22	in
Sleeve seam	25	31	35	40	43	cm
	10	12¼	13¾	15¾	17	in

To fit adult sizes	small	medium	large	extra large	
Actual chest/bust	114	120	128	134	cm
measurement	45	47¼	50½	52¾	in
Length	62	66	69	71	cm
	24½	26	27	28	in
Sleeve seam	46	46	51	51	cm
	18	18	20	20	in

MATERIALS

4(5:6:7:8:10:11:13:13) 50g balls of Rowan DK Handknit Cotton in Burgundy (A).

1(1:2:2:2:2:2:3:3) balls of same in each of Red, Purple, Navy, Green, Lime and Light Blue.

1 ball of same in Cream.

Pair each of 3¼mm (No 10/US 3) and 4mm (No 8/US 6) knitting needles.

TENSION

23 sts and 25 rows to 10cm/4in square over pattern on 4mm (No 8/US 6) needles.

ABBREVIATIONS

See page 7.

NOTE

Read chart from right to left on right side (k) rows and from left to right on wrong side (p) rows. When working in pattern, strand yarn not in use loosely across wrong side to keep fabric elastic.

BACK

With 3¼mm (No 10/US 3) needles and A, cast on 79(87:95:103:111:121:127:135:143) sts.

1st row K1, [p1, k1] to end.

This row forms moss st. Moss st 6(6:6:8:8:8:10:10:10) rows more.

Inc row Moss st 6(5:3:7:6:6:8:7:5), *m1, moss st 6(7:8:8:9:12:10:11:12); rep from * to last 7(5:4:8:6:7:9:7:6) sts, m1, moss st to end. 91(99:107:115:123:131:139:147:155) sts.

Change to 4mm (No 8/US 6) needles. Beg with a k row, work in st st and patt from chart until Back measures 37(42:46:52:56:62:66:69:71)cm/14½(16½:18:20½:22:24½:26:27:28)in from beg, ending with a wrong side row.

Shape Shoulders

Cast off 14(16:18:19:21:23:24:26:28) sts at beg of next 2 rows and 15(16:18:20:22:23:25:26:28) sts at beg of foll 2 rows. Leave rem 33(35:35:37:37:39:41:43:43) sts on a holder.

FRONT

Work as given for Back until Front measures 32(36:40:46:49:55:59:61:63)cm/12½(14¼:15¾:18:19¼:21¾:23¼:24:25)in from beg, ending with a wrong side row.

Shape Neck

Next row Patt 37(40:44:47:51:54:57:61:65), turn.

Work on this set of sts only. Keeping patt correct, dec one st at neck edge on next 6 rows then on every foll alt row until 29(32:36:39:43:46:49:52:56) sts rem. Cont straight until Front matches Back to shoulder shaping, ending at side edge.

Shape Shoulder

Cast off 14(16:18:19:21:23:24:26:28) sts at beg of next row. Work 1 row. Cast off rem 15(16:18:20:22:23:25:26:28) sts.

With right side facing, slip centre 17(19:19:21:21:23:25:25:25) sts onto a holder, rejoin yarn to rem sts and patt to end. Complete as first side.

SLEEVES

With 3¼mm (No 10/US 3) needles and A, cast on 37(39:41:43:43:45:45:47:47) sts. Work 13(13:13:13:13:17:17:17:17) rows in moss st as given for Back.

Inc row Moss st 3(3:2:4:4:3:3:1:1), *m1, moss st 6(3:4:5:5:3:3:4:4); rep from * to last 4(3:3:4:4:3:3:2:2) sts, m1, moss st to end. 43(51:51:51:51:59:59:59:59) sts.

Change to 4mm (No 8/US 6) needles. Beg with a k row, work in st st and patt from chart, inc one st at each end of 5th row and every foll 3rd(5th:4th:4th:4th:4th:4th:4th:4th) row until there are 67(73:81:85:89:95:99:103:109) sts, working inc sts into patt. Cont straight until Sleeve measures 25(31:35:40:43:46:46:51:51)cm/10(12¼:13¾:15¾:17:18:18:20:20)in from beg, ending with a wrong side row. Cast off.

NECKBAND

Join right shoulder seam.
With 3¼mm (No 10/US 3) needles, A and right side facing, k up 14(16:16:16:18:18:18:20:20) sts down left front neck, k centre front sts, k up 14(16:16:16:18:18:18:20:20) sts up right front neck, k back neck sts dec one st at centre.
77(85:85:89:93:97:101:107:107) sts.
1st row P1, [k1, p1] to end.
2nd row K1, [p1, k1] to end.
Rep last 2 rows 3(3:3:4:4:4:5:5:5) times.
Work 9(9:9:11:11:11:13:13:13) rows in moss st as given for Back. Cast off loosely.

TO MAKE UP

Join left shoulder and neckband seam, reversing seam on moss stitch section of neckband. Sew on sleeves, placing centre of sleeves to shoulder seams. Join side and sleeve seams.

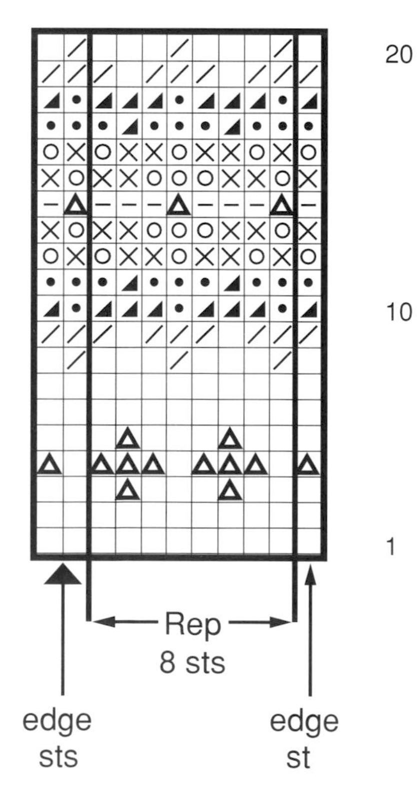

☐ = Burgundy (A)
Δ = Red
⁄ = Purple
◢ = Navy
• = Green
○ = Lime
⊠ = Light Blue
⊟ = Cream

Shawl collar fairisle jacket

This jacket has subtly shading fairisle bands and an integrated patterned collar. My fondness for this design is in no way influenced by the fact that it is worn by my daughter Eleanor!

MEASUREMENTS

To fit ages/sizes	3-4yrs	5-6yrs	7-8yrs	9-10yrs	small	medium	large	
Actual chest/bust	81	88	94	101	121	128	134	cm
measurement	32	34½	37	39½	47½	50½	52¾	in
Length	46	50	54	60	74	75	76	cm
	18	19¾	21¼	23½	29	29½	30	in
Sleeve seam	28	31	35	38	44	45	46	cm
	11	12¼	13¾	15	17¼	17¾	18	in

MATERIALS

4(4:5:5:6:7:8) 100g hanks of Rowan Magpie in Deep Green (A).
1(1:1:2:2:2:2) hanks of same in Mid Green.
1(1:1:1:2:2:2) hanks of same in Light Green.
1(1:1:1:1:2:2) hanks of same in Gold.
1 hank of same in each of Natural, Mid Red and Deep Red.
2(2:2:3:3:3:4) 50g balls of Rowan Designer DK Wool in Brown and 1 ball in Cream (this yarn is used double throughout).
Pair each of 4mm (No 8/US 6) and 5mm (No 6/US 8) knitting needles.
4(4:5:5:6:6:6) buttons.

TENSION

18 sts and 21 rows to 10cm/4in square over pattern on 5mm (No 6/US 8) needles.

ABBREVIATIONS

See page 7.

NOTES

Read chart from right to left on right side (k) rows and from left to right on wrong side (p) rows. When working in pattern, strand yarn not in use loosely across wrong side to keep fabric elastic.

BACK

With 4mm (No 8/US 6) needles and A, cast on 73(79:85:91:109:115:121) sts.
Beg with a p row, work 6 rows in st st.
K 1 row for fold line.
Change to 5mm (No 6/US 8) needles.
Beg with a k row, work 6 rows in st st.
Cont in st st and beg with 1st(1st:1st:1st:35th:35th:35th) row, work in patt from chart until Back measures 45(49:53:59:73:74:75)cm/17¾(19½:21:23¼:28¾:29¼:29¾)in from fold line, ending with a right side row.

Shape Neck and Shoulders

Next row Patt 29(32:34:36:44:47:49), cast off next 15(15:17:19:21:21:23) sts, patt to end.
Work on last set of sts only. Patt 1 row.
Cast off 3 sts at beg of next row. Cast off rem 26(29:31:33:41:44:46) sts.
With right side facing, rejoin yarn to rem sts, cast off 3 sts, patt to end. Patt 1 row. Cast off rem 26(29:31:33:41:44:46) sts.

POCKET LININGS (MAKE 2)

With 5mm (No 6/US 8) needles and A, cast on 18(18:20:20:22:22:24) sts.
Beg with a k row, work 20(20:22:22:24:24:26) rows in st st. Leave these sts on a holder.

LEFT FRONT

With 4mm (No 8/US 6) needles and A, cast on 42(45:48:51:60:63:66) sts.
Work as given for Back until Front measures 12(14:16:18:20:21:22)cm/4¾(5½:6¼:7:8:8¼:8¾)in from folding line, ending with a wrong side row.

Place Pocket

Next row Patt 9(10:10:12:15:17:17), slip next 18(18:20:20:22:22:24) sts onto a holder, patt across sts of pocket lining, patt to end.
Cont in patt until work measures 32(33:34:37:48:48:48)cm/12½(13:13½:14½:19:19:19)in from folding line, ending at front edge.

Shape Neck

Cast off 9 sts at beg of next row.
Keeping patt correct, dec one st at neck edge on 3rd row and every foll 4th row until 26(29:31:33:41:44:46) sts rem. Cont straight until Front measures same as Back to cast off edge, ending with a wrong side row. Cast off.
Mark front edge to indicate buttons: first one 8(9:6:9:8:8:8)cm/3(3½:2½:3½:3:3:3)in from fold line, last one 1.5cm/½in below neck shaping and rem 2(2:3:3:4:4:4) evenly spaced between.

RIGHT FRONT

Work as given for Left Front until Front measures 8(9:6:9:8:8:8)cm/3(3½:2½:3½:3:3:3)in from fold line, ending with a wrong side row.
Buttonhole row (right side) Patt 3, k2 tog, yf, patt to end.
Complete as given for Left Front, working buttonholes to match markers, reversing neck shaping and placing

Cream Denim Tunic with Pockets

Knitted in a beautiful cream denim yarn, which shrinks to the required measurements after the first wash, this design is longline, with a centre cable that integrates down into the deep patterned welt.

MATERIALS
29(30:31) 50g balls of Rowan Denim.
Pair each of 3¾mm (No 9/US 4) and 4mm (No 8/US 6) knitting needles.
Cable needle.

MEASUREMENTS
The following measurements are after the garment has been washed according to the instructions on the ball band.

To fit bust	small	medium	large
Actual bust measurement	114 45	124 48¾	134cm 52¾in
Length	71 28	73 28¾	75cm 29½in
Sleeve seam	46 18	46 18	46cm 18 in

TENSION
20 sts and 28 rows to 10cm/4in square over st st on 4mm (No 8/US 6) needles before washing.
16 sts of panel A pattern measures 16cm/6¼in, 24 sts of panel B pattern measures 9cm/3½in and 20 sts of panel C pattern measures 7.5cm/3in.

ABBREVIATIONS
C4B = sl next 2 sts onto cable needle and leave at back of work, k2, then k2 from cable needle;
C4F = sl next 2 sts onto cable needle and leave at front of work, k2, then k2 from cable needle;
Cr2L = sl next st onto cable needle and leave at front of work, p1, then k st from cable needle;
Cr2R = sl next st onto cable needle and leave at back of work, k1, then p st from cable needle;
Cr3L = sl next 2 sts onto cable needle and leave at front of work, p1, then k2 from cable needle;
Cr3R = sl next st onto cable needle and leave at back of work, k2, then p st from cable needle;
mb = pick up loop lying between st just worked and next st, work into back, front and back of the loop, turn, p3, turn, k3, turn, p1, p2 tog, turn, k2 tog.
Also see page 7.

PANEL A
Worked over 40 sts.
1st row (right side) P3, mb, p1, pass bobble st over p st just worked, p2, k4, [p4, mb, p1, pass bobble st over the p st just worked, p3, k4] twice, p3, mb, p1, pass bobble st over p st just worked, p2.
2nd row K6, p4, [k8, p4] twice, k6.
3rd row P6, C4B, [p8, C4B] twice, p6.
4th row As 2nd row.
5th row P5, Cr3R, Cr3L, [p6, Cr3R, Cr3L] twice, p5.
6th row K5, p2, k2, p2, [k6, p2, k2, p2] twice, k5.
7th row P4, [Cr3R, p2, Cr3L, p4] 3 times.
8th row K4, [p2, k4] 6 times.
9th row P3, Cr3R, p4, Cr3L, [p2, Cr3R, p4, Cr3L] twice, p3.
10th row K3, p2, k6, p2, [k2, p2, k6, p2] twice, k3.
11th row P2, [Cr3R, p6, Cr3L] 3 times, p2.
12th row K2, [p2, k8, p2] 3 times, k2.
13th row P2, k2, p8, [C4B, p8] twice, k2, p2.
14th row As 12th row.
15th row P2, k2, p4, mb, p1, pass bobble st over p st just worked, p3, [k4, p4, mb, p1, pass bobble st over p st just worked, p3] twice, k2, p2.
16th to 18th rows Work 12th to 14th rows.
19th row P2, [Cr3L, p6, Cr3R] 3 times, p2.
20th row As 10th row.
21st row P3, Cr3L, p4, Cr3R, [p2, Cr3L, p4, Cr3R] twice, p3.
22nd row As 8th row.
23rd row P4, [Cr3L, p2, Cr3R, p4] 3 times.
24th row As 6th row.
25th row P5, Cr3L, Cr3R, [p6, Cr3L, Cr3R] twice, p5.
26th to 28th rows Work 2nd to 4th rows.
These 28 rows form patt.

PANEL B
Worked over 24 sts.
1st row (right side) P4, Cr3R, p2, Cr3R, Cr3L, p2, Cr3L, p4.
2nd row K4, p2, k3, p2, k2, p2, k3, p2, k4.
3rd row P3, [Cr3R, p2] twice, Cr3L, p2, Cr3L, p3.
4th row [K3, p2] twice, k4, [p2, k3] twice.
5th row P2, [Cr3R, p2] twice, mb, p1, pass bobble st over p st just worked, p1, [Cr3L, p2] twice.
6th row K2, p2, k3, p2, k6, p2, k3, p2, k2.
7th row [P2, Cr3L] twice, p4, [Cr3R, p2] twice.
8th row As 4th row.
9th row P3, [Cr3L, p2] twice, Cr3R, p2, Cr3R, p3.
10th row As 2nd row.
11th row P4, Cr3L, p2, Cr3L, Cr3R, p2, Cr3R, p4.
12th row K5, p2, k3, p4, k3, p2, k5.
These 12 rows form patt.

HERRINGBONE DENIM SWEATER

A simple sweater with a herringbone stitch yoke and knitted in the denim yarn. Pictured opposite on Donal in cream, it is worn by babies Cairo and Max on pages 28 and 33 in the blue shade, which fades beautifully when washed and worn.

MATERIALS
6(8:10:12:14:16:21:22:23:24) 50g balls of Rowan Denim.
Pair each of 3¼mm (No 10/US 3) and 4mm (No 8/US 6) knitting needles.

TENSION
20 sts and 28 rows to 10cm/4in square over st st on 4mm (No 8/US 6) needles before washing.

ABBREVIATIONS
See page 7.

MEASUREMENTS
The following measurements are after the garment has been washed according to the instructions given on ball band.

To fit ages	1-2yrs	2-4yrs	4-6yrs	6-8yrs	8-10yrs	10-12yrs	
Actual chest/bust	65	77	85	97	105	113	cm
measurement	25½	30¼	33½	38	41¼	44½	in
Length	32	39	44	52	56	58	cm
	12½	15½	17¼	20½	22	22¾	in
Sleeve seam	22	28	32	36	44	46	cm
	8¾	11	12½	14¼	17¼	18	in

To fit adult sizes	small	medium	large	extra large	
Actual chest/bust	117	125	129	137	cm
measurement	46	49	50¾	54	in
Length	62	64	66	66	cm
	24½	25¼	26	26	in
Sleeve seam	48	48	52	52	cm
	19	19	20½	20½	in

BACK
With 3¼mm (No 10/US 3) needles cast on 62(74:82:94:102:110:114:122:126:134) sts.
1st rib row (right side) K2, [p2, k2] to end.
2nd rib row P2, [k2, p2] to end.
Rep last 2 rows 5(5:5:7:7:7:9:9:9:9) times, inc 3 sts evenly across last row. 65(77:85:97:105:113:117:125:129:137) sts.
Change to 4mm (No 8/US 6) needles.
Beg with a k row, work in st st until Back measures 23(25:29:36:39:39:42:45:45:45)cm/9(10:11½:14¼:15½:15½:16½:17¾:17¾:17¾)in from beg, ending with a p row.
Work in patt from chart until Back measures 38(47:53:63:68:70:75:78:80:80)cm/15(18½:21:24¾:26¾:27½:29½:30¾:31½:31½)in from beg, ending with a wrong side row.
Shape Neck
Next row Patt 22(27:30:35:39:42:44:47:49:52), turn.
Work on this set of sts only. Dec one st at neck edge on next 4 rows. 18(23:26:31:35:38:40:43:45:48) sts. Work 1 row.
Shape Shoulders
Cast off 6(8:8:10:11:12:13:14:15:16) sts at beg of next row and foll alt row.
Work 1 row. Cast off rem 6(7:10:11:13:14:14:15:15:16) sts.
With right side facing, slip centre 21(23:25:27:27:29:29:31:31:33) sts onto a holder, rejoin yarn to rem sts and patt to end. Complete to match first side.

FRONT
Work as given for Back until Front is 14(16:18:20:22:22:24:24:26:26) rows less than Back to shoulder shaping, ending with a wrong side row.
Shape Neck
Next row Patt 27(32:35:40:44:47:49:52: 54:57), turn.
Work on this set of sts only. Dec one st at neck edge on next 8(6:4:4:2:2:2:2:2:2) rows then on every alt row until 18(23:26:31:35:38:40:43:45:48) sts rem.
Cont straight until Front matches Back to shoulder shaping, ending at side edge.
Shape Shoulder
Cast off 6(8:8:10:11:12:13:14:15:16) sts at beg of next row and foll alt row.
Work 1 row. Cast off rem 6(7:10:11:13:14:14:15:15:16) sts.
With right side facing, slip centre 11(13:15:17:17:19:19:21:21:23) sts onto a holder, rejoin yarn to rem sts and patt to end. Complete as given for first side.

SLEEVES
With 3¼mm (No 10/US 3) needles cast on 38(42:46:50:54:54:58:58:62:62) sts. Work 12(12:14:14:16:16:20:20:20:

THE WELL-VERSED CAT

20) rows in rib as given for Back welt. Change to 4mm (No 8/US 6) needles. Beg with a k row, work in st st, inc one st at each end of 5th(5th:5th:3rd:3rd:3rd:3rd:3rd:3rd:3rd) row and every foll 4th(4th:4th:5th:6th:5th:5th:6th:6th:6th) row until there are 64(74:82:88:94:100:106:106:112:112) sts. Cont straight until Sleeve measures 27(35:40:45:55:57:60:60:65:65)cm/10½(13¾:15¾:17¾:21½:22½:23½:23½:25½:25½)in from beg, ending with a wrong side row. Cast off.

NECKBAND

Join right shoulder seam. With 3¼mm (No 10/US 3) needles and right side facing, k up 18(20:22:24:26:26:28:30:32:32) sts down left front neck, k centre front sts, k up 18(20:22:24:26:26:28:30:32:32) sts up right front neck, 9 sts down right back neck, k back neck sts, k up 9 sts up left back neck. 86(94:102:110:114:118:122:130:134:138) sts. Work 9(9:11:11:11:11:13:13:13:13) rows in rib as given for Back welt. ** Cast off in rib.

POLO COLLAR

Work as given for Neckband to **. Change to 4mm (No 8/US 6) needles. Rib a further 10(10:12:12:14:14:16:16:18:18) rows. Cast off in rib.

TO MAKE UP

Join left shoulder and neckband or collar seam, reversing seam half way on polo collar. Wash all pieces according to the instructions on the ball band. When dry, sew on sleeves, placing centre of sleeves to shoulder seams. Join side and sleeve seams. If desired, leave side seams open on welts.

Key

☐ = K on right side
P on wrong side

 = P on right side
K on wrong side

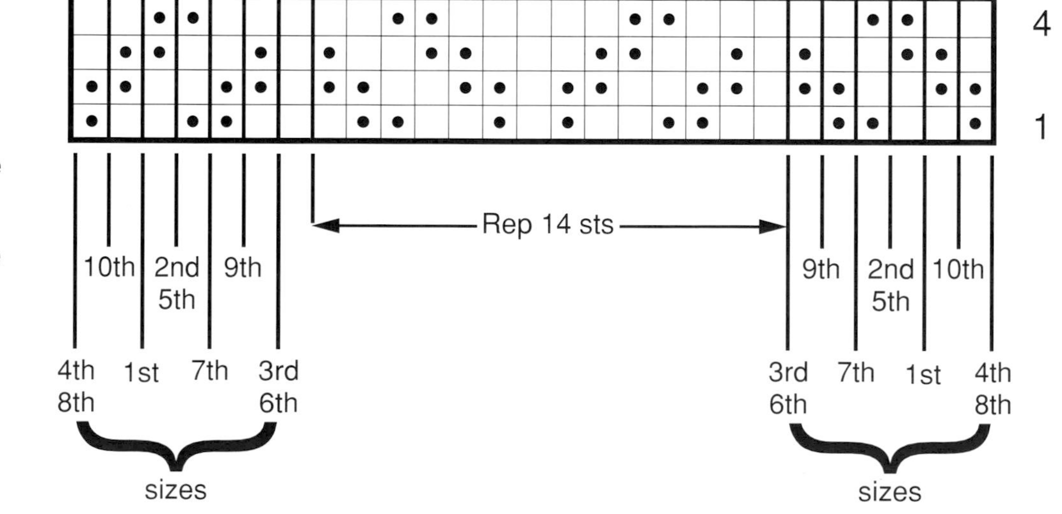

DIAMOND AND ZIGZAG DENIM SWEATER

This design uses classic guernsey stitch patterns and is shown in both the black and blue shades. The more the garments are washed, the better the designs look, as the fading produces beautiful shaded effects on the stitches.

MATERIALS
12(16:20:24:27) 50g balls of Rowan Denim.
Pair each of 3¾mm (No 9/US 4) and 4mm (No 8/US 6) knitting needles.

TENSION
20 sts and 28 rows to 10cm/4in square over st st on 4mm (No 8/US 6) needles before washing.

ABBREVIATIONS
See page 7.

NOTE
Read charts from right to left on right side rows and from left to right on wrong side rows.

BACK AND FRONT (ALIKE)
With 3¾mm (No 9/US 4) needles, cast on 87(105:119:137:151) sts.
1st rib row (right side) K0(1:0:1:0), p3, [k1, p3] to last 0(1:0:1:0) st, k0(1:0:1:0).
2nd rib row P0(1:0:1:0), k1, [p1, k1] to last 0(1:0:1:0) st, p0(1:0:1:0).
These 2 rows form rib. Rep last 2 rows until welt measures 18(20:22:27:30)cm/ 7(8:8½:10½:12)in, ending with a 2nd row.
Change to 4mm (No 8/US 6) needles.
1st row Rib 7(0:7:0:7), [work 1st row of chart 2, rib 7] 0(1:1:0:0) time, [work 1st row of chart 1, rib 7, work 1st row of chart 2, rib 7] to last 16(25:32:9:16) sts, work 1st row of chart 1, [rib 7, work 1st row of chart 2] 0(1:1:0:0) time, rib 7(0:7:0:7).
This row sets position of panel patt from charts with rib panels in between.
Cont in patt until Back measures 46(54: 62:75:77)cm/18(21¼:24½:29½:30½)in

MEASUREMENTS
The following measurements are after the garment has been washed according to the instructions on ball band.

To fit ages/sizes	3-4yrs	6-8yrs	8-10yrs	small-medium	medium-large	
Actual chest/bust	81	98	110	127	140	cm
measurement	32	38½	43	50	55	in
Length	42	48	55	65	67	cm
	16½	19	21½	25½	26½	in
Sleeve seam	28	36	40	48	54	cm
	11	14	15¾	19	21¼	in

Diamond and Zigzag Denim Sweater (left) and Herringbone Denim Sweater (see page 30).

from beg, ending with a wrong side row.

Shape Shoulders

Cast off 11(14:16:13:14) sts at beg of next 6(6:6:8:8) rows. Leave rem 21(21: 23:33:39) sts on a holder.

SLEEVES

With 3¾mm (No 9/US 4) needles cast on 47(49:51:53:55) sts.

1st rib row (right side) P3(0:1:2:3), k1, [p3, k1] to last 3(0:1:2:3) sts, p3(0:1: 2:3).

2nd rib row K1(0:1:0:1), p1, [k1, p1] to last 1(0:1:0:1) st, k1(0:1:0:1).

These 2 rows form rib. Rep last 2 rows until cuff measures 7(8:8:10:10)cm/2¾ (3:3:4:4)in, ending with a 2nd row.

Change to 4mm (No 8/US 6) needles.

1st row Rib 3(4:5:6:7), work 1st row of chart 1, rib 7, work 1st row of chart 2, rib 7, work 1st row of chart 1, rib 3(4:5:6:7).

This row sets position of panel patt from charts with rib panels in between.

Cont in patt, inc one st at each end of 2nd row and every foll 5th row until there are 73(81:93:101:111) sts, working inc sts into patt. Cont straight until Sleeve measures 35(45:50:60: 67)cm/13¾(17¾:19¾:23¾:26½)in from beg, ending with a wrong side row.

Shape Saddle Shoulder

Cast off 25(29:35:39:44) sts at beg of next 2 rows. Cont straight on rem 23 sts until saddle measures 13(18:20:21: 24)cm/5(7:8:8¼:9½)in, ending with a wrong side row.

Shape Neck

Next row Patt 8(8:8:10:10), turn.

Work on this set of sts only. Dec one st at inside edge on next row and every foll alt row until 2 sts rem. Work 2 tog and fasten off.

With right side facing, slip centre 7(7:7:3:3) sts onto a holder, rejoin yarn to rem sts and patt to end. Complete as first side.

NECKBAND

Sew both front saddles and right back saddle in position.

With 3¼mm (No 10/US 3) needles and right side facing, k up 11(11:11:15:15) sts down first side of left sleeve saddle, k centre sts, k up 11(11:11:14:15) sts up other side of saddle, k centre front sts, k up 10(10:11:14:15) sts up first side of right sleeve saddle, k centre sts, k up 10(10:11:14:15) sts up other side of saddle, k centre back sts. 98(98:104: 129:144) sts.

1st rib row P1(1:0:1:0), k1, [p1, k1] to last 0(0:1:1:1) st, p0(0:1:1:1).

2nd rib row K0(0:1:1:1), [p3, k1] to last 2(2:3:0:3) sts, p2(2:3:0:3).

Rep last 2 rows 4(4:4:5:5) times more, then work 1st row again. Beg with a k row, work 6 rows in st st. Cast off loosely.

TO MAKE UP

Sew remaining saddle and neckband seam. Wash the garment according to the instructions given on ball band. When dry, sew remainder of sleeves in place. Join side and sleeve seams.

Chart 1

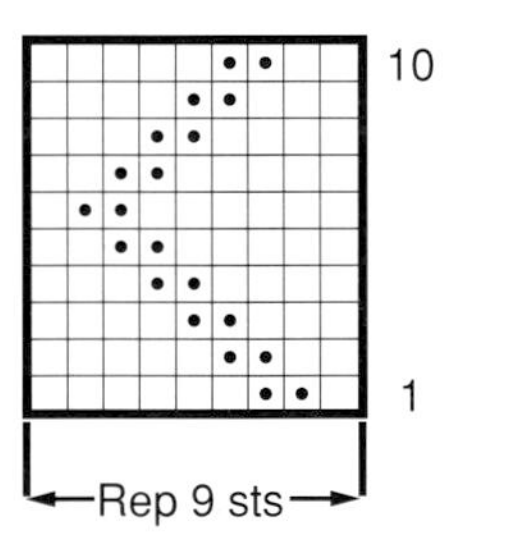

Chart 2

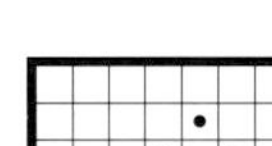

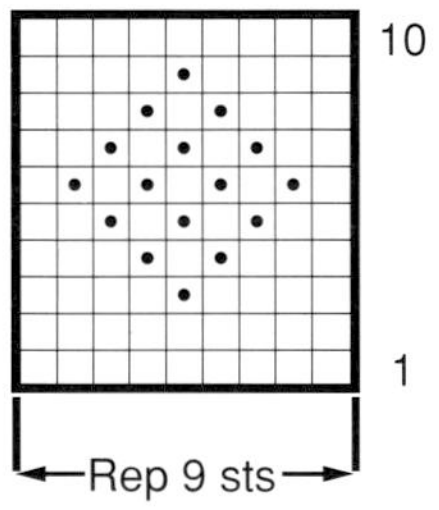

Key

□ = K on right side
P on wrong side

⊡ = P on right side
K on wrong side

Denim lace

In this design I have mixed zigzag cables with lace and bobble panels. The deep cable and faggot stitch welts give a delicate scalloped effect to the body, neckband and sleeves.

MATERIALS
24(27:29:31) 50g balls of Rowan Denim.
Pair each of 3¼mm (No 10/US 3), 3¾mm (No 9/US 4) and 4mm (No 8/US 6) knitting needles.
Cable needle.

TENSION
20 sts and 28 rows to 10cm/4in square over st st on 4mm (No 8/US 6) needles before washing.
12 sts of panel A or D pattern measures 3.5cm/1½in and 49 sts of panel C pattern measures 17cm/6¾in.

MEASUREMENTS
The following measurements are after the garment has been washed according to the instructions on ball band.

To fit age/sizes	4-6yrs	9-11yrs	small-medium	medium-large	
Actual chest/bust measurement	90	108	124	138	cm
	35½	42½	49	54½	in
Length	48	56	70	76	cm
	19	22	27½	30	in
Sleeve seam	31	43	52	56	cm
	12¼	17	20½	22	in

ABBREVIATIONS
C2B = sl next st onto cable needle and leave at back of work, p1, then p st from cable needle;
C2F = sl next st onto cable needle and leave at front of work, p1, then p st from cable needle;
C3B = sl next st onto cable needle and leave at back of work, k2, then k st from cable needle;
C3F = sl next 2 sts onto cable needle and leave at front of work, k1, then k2 from cable needle;
C4B = sl next 2 sts onto cable needle and leave at back of work, k2, then k2 from cable needle;
C4F = sl next 2 sts onto cable needle and leave at front of work, k2, then k2 from cable needle;
C5 = sl next 3 sts onto cable needle and leave at back of work, k2, sl first st on cable needle back onto left hand needle, k this st, then k2 from cable needle;
C6B = sl next 3 sts onto cable needle and leave at back of work, k3, then k3 from cable needle;
C6F = sl next 3 sts onto cable needle and leave at front of work, k3, then k3 from cable needle;
Cr2L = sl next st onto cable needle and leave at front of work, p1, then k st from cable needle;
Cr2R = sl next st onto cable needle and leave at back of work, k1, then p st from cable needle;
Cr3L = sl next 2 sts onto cable needle and leave at front of work, p1, then k2 from cable needle;
Cr3R = sl next st onto cable needle and leave at back of work, k2, then p st from cable needle;
Cr4L = sl next 2 sts onto cable needle and leave at front of work, p1, k1, then k2 from cable needle;
Cr4R = sl next 2 sts onto cable needle and leave at back of work, k2, then k1, p1 from cable needle;
Tw4L = sl next 2 sts onto cable needle and leave at front of work, k1, p1, then k2 from cable needle;
Tw4R = sl next 2 sts onto cable needle and leave at back of work, k2, then p1, k1 from cable needle;
mb = make bobble, [k1, p1, k1, p1] all in next st, turn, p4, turn, [k2 tog] twice, then pass second st over first st.
Also see page 7.

PANEL A
Worked over 12 sts.
1st row (wrong side) P2, [k1, p1] 5 times.
2nd row [K1, p1] 4 times, Cr4R.
3rd row K1, p3, [k1, p1] 4 times.
4th row [K1, p1] 3 times, Cr4R, Cr2L.
5th row P1, k2, p3, [k1, p1] 3 times.
6th row [K1, p1] twice, Cr4R, Cr2L, Cr2R.
7th row K1, C2B, k2, p3, [k1, p1] twice.
8th row K1, p1, Cr4R, Cr2L, Cr2R, Cr2L.
9th row P1, k2, C2F, k2, p3, k1, p1.
10th row Cr4R, [Cr2L, Cr2R] twice.
11th row K1, [C2B, k2] twice, p3.
12th row Tw4L, [Cr2R, Cr2L] twice.
13th row As 9th row.
14th row K1, p1, Tw4L, Cr2R, Cr2L, Cr2R.
15th row As 7th row.
16th row [K1, p1] twice, Tw4L, Cr2R, Cr2L.

CABLE AND MOSS STITCH JACKET AND TUNIC

This jacket is knitted in a subtly flecked tweedy yarn, and has a wide ribbed collar. It is also featured in the tunic style on model Susie on page 45, pictured with sons Oscar and Cairo.

MATERIALS

Jacket 20(21:22) 50g balls of Rowan DK Tweed.
Medium size crochet hook.
Tunic 18(19:20) 50g balls of Rowan DK Tweed.
Both designs Pair each of 3¼mm (No 10/US 3), 3¾mm (No 9/US 4) and 4mm (No 8/US 6) knitting needles.
Cable needle.

MEASUREMENTS

To fit sizes	small-medium	medium-large	large-extra large	
Actual bust	122	136	151	cm
measurement	48	53½	59½	in
Length	72	75	78	cm
	28¼	29½	30¾	in
Sleeve seam	46	46	46	cm
(with cuff turned back)	18	18	18	in

TENSION

26 sts and 34 rows to 10cm/4in square over moss stitch and cable pattern on 4mm (No 8/US 6) needles.

ABBREVIATIONS

See page 7.

JACKET

BACK

With 3¾mm (No 9/US 4) needles cast on 134(150:166) sts.
1st rib row (right side) K2, [p2, k2] to end.
2nd rib row P2, [k2, p2] to end.
Rep last 2 rows until welt measures 10cm/4in, ending with a right side row.
Inc row Rib 3, [m1, rib 7, m1, rib 2, m1, rib 7] to last 3 sts, m1, rib 3. 159(178:197) sts.
Change to 4mm (No 8/US 6) needles.
1st row (right side) K1, [p1, k1] 3 times, * p2, [k1, p1] twice, k4, p2, k1, [p1, k1] 3 times; rep from * to end.
2nd row K1, [p1, k1] 3 times, * k2, p5, k1, p1, k4, [p1, k1] 3 times; rep from * to end.
3rd and 4th rows As 1st and 2nd rows.
5th row K1, [p1, k1] 3 times, * p2, sl next 4 sts onto cable needle and leave at back of work, k4, then [k1, p1] twice from cable needle, p2, k1, [p1, k1] 3 times; rep from * to end.
6th row K1, [p1, k1] 3 times, * k2, [p1, k1] twice, p4, k3, [p1, k1] 3 times; rep from * to end.
7th row K1, [p1, k1] 3 times, * p2, k5, p1, k1, p3, k1, [p1, k1] 3 times; rep from * to end.
8th row As 6th row.
9th to 14th rows Work 7th and 8th rows 3 times.
15th row K1, [p1, k1] 3 times, * p2, sl next 4 sts onto cable needle and leave at back of work, [k1, p1] twice, then k4 from cable needle, p2, k1, [p1, k1] 3 times; rep from * to end.
16th row As 2nd row.
17th to 20th rows Work 1st and 2nd rows twice.
These 20 rows form moss st and cable patt. Cont in patt until work measures 72(75:78)cm/28¼(29½:30¾)in from beg, ending with a wrong side row.
Shape Shoulders
Cast off 28(32:36) sts at beg of next 2 rows and 28(33:37) sts at beg of foll 2 rows. Cast off rem 47(48:51) sts.

LEFT POCKET LINING

With 4mm (No 8/US 6) needles cast on 32(33:34) sts. Work 15cm/6in in st st, ending with a k row.
Inc row P2(7:12), m1, p2, m1, p15, m1, p2, m1, p11(7:3). 36(37:38) sts.
Leave these sts on a holder.

LEFT FRONT

With 3¾mm (No 9/US 4) needles cast on 70(80:86) sts.
1st rib row (right side) [K2, p2] to last 2(0:2) sts, k2(0:2).
2nd rib row P2(0:2), [k2, p2] to end.
Rep last 2 rows until welt measures 10cm/4in, ending with a right side row.
Inc row [Rib 3, m1, rib 3] 1(0:1) time, [rib 4, m1, rib 2, m1, rib 7, m1, rib 3] to end. 83(95:102) sts.
Change to 4mm (No 8/US 6) needles.
1st row (right side) * K1, [p1, k1] 3 times, p2, [k1, p1] twice, k4, p2; rep from * to last 7(0:7) sts, k1(0:1), [p1, k1] 3(0:3) times.
2nd row K1(0:1), [p1, k1] 3(0:3) times, *k2, p5, k1, p1, k4, [p1, k1] 3 times; rep from * to end.
These 2 rows set position of moss st and cable patt. Cont in patt to match Back until Front measures 22(23:

24)cm/8¾(9:9½)in from beg, ending with a wrong side row.

Place Pocket

Next row Patt 19(23:27), slip next 36(37:38) sts onto a holder, patt across sts of pocket lining, patt to end.

Cont in patt until Front measures 40 (43:46)cm/15¾(17:18)in from beg, ending with a wrong side row.

Shape Neck

Keeping patt correct, dec one st at neck edge on next row and every foll 3rd row until 56(65:73) sts rem. Patt 7(0:0) rows. Mark last row at neck edge. Cont straight until Front matches Back to shoulder shaping, ending at side edge.

Shape Shoulder

Cast off 28(32:36) sts at beg of next row. Work 1 row. Cast off rem 28(33: 37) sts.

RIGHT POCKET LINING

Work as Left Pocket Lining, reversing inc row as follows:

Inc row P11(7:3), m1, p2, m1, p15, m1, p2, m1, p2(7:12).

RIGHT FRONT

With 3¾mm (No 9/US 4) needles cast on 70(80:86) sts.

1st rib row (right side) K2(0:2), [p2, k2] to end.

2nd rib row [P2, k2] to last 2(0:2) sts, p2(0:2).

Rep last 2 rows until welt measures 10cm/4in, ending with a right side row.

Inc row [Rib 3, m1, rib 7, m1, rib 2, m1, rib 4] to last 6(0:6) sts, [rib 3, m1, rib 3] 1(0:1) time. 83(95:102) sts.

Change to 4mm (No 8/US 6) needles.

1st row (right side) K1(0:1), [p1, k1] 3(0:3) times, * p2, [k1, p1] twice, k4, p2, k1, [p1, k1] 3 times; rep from * to end.

2nd row * [K1, p1] 3 times, k3, p5, k1, p1, k3; rep from * to last 7(0:7) sts, k1(0:1), [p1, k1] 3(0:3) times.

These 2 rows set position of moss st and cable patt. Complete as Left Front reversing pocket placing as follows:

Next row Patt 28(35:37), slip next 36(37:38) sts onto a holder, patt across sts of pocket lining, patt to end.

SLEEVES

With 3¾mm (No 9/US 4) needles cast on 54 sts. Work 12cm/4¾in in rib as given for Back, ending with a right side row.

Inc row Rib 3, [m1, rib 7, m1, rib 2, m1, rib 7] to last 3 sts, m1, rib 3. 64 sts.

Change to 4mm (No 8/US 6) needles. Work in patt as given for Back, inc one st at each end of 3rd row and every foll 5th(4th:4th) row until there are 110(116:120) sts, working inc sts into moss st patt. Cont straight until Sleeve measures 52cm/20½in from beg, ending with a wrong side row. Cast off.

POCKET TOPS

With 3¼mm (No 10/US 3) needles and right side facing, rejoin yarn to sts on holder, patt 1 row, dec 1 st over each moss st section and 2 sts over each cable. 30(32:32) sts.

1st rib row K0(1:1), p2, [k2, p2] to last 0(1:1) st, k0(1:1).

2nd rib row P0(1:1), k2, [p2, k2] to last 0(1:1) st, p0(1:1).

Rep last 2 rows 4 times more. Cast off in rib.

RIGHT FRONT BAND AND COLLAR

With 3¼mm (No 10/US 3) needles and right side facing, k up 108(116:124) sts along right front edge to beg of neck shaping and 66 sts along shaped edge to marker. 174(182:190) sts. Beg with a 2nd row, work 2 rows in rib as given for Back.

Next 2 rows Rib 58, yb, sl 1, yf, turn, sl 1, rib to end.

Next 2 rows Rib 54, yb, sl 1, yf, turn, sl 1, rib to end.

Next 2 rows Rib 50, yb, sl 1, yf, turn, sl 1, rib to end.

Next 2 rows Rib 46, yb, sl 1, yf, turn, sl 1, rib to end.

Next 2 rows Rib 42, yb, sl 1, yf, turn, sl 1, rib to end.

Rib a further 28 rows across all sts. Cast off in rib.

LEFT FRONT BAND AND COLLAR

With 3¼mm (No 10/US 3) needles, right side facing and beg at marker, k up 66 sts along shaped edge of left front to beg of neck shaping and 108(116: 124) sts along straight edge to cast on edge. 174(182:190) sts. Beg with a 2nd row, work 1 row in rib as given for Back.

Next 2 rows Rib 58, yf, sl 1, yb, turn, sl 1, rib to end.

Next 2 rows Rib 54, yf, sl 1, yb, turn, sl 1, rib to end.

Next 2 rows Rib 50, yf, sl 1, yb, turn, sl 1, rib to end.

Next 2 rows Rib 46, yf, sl 1, yb, turn, sl 1, rib to end.

Next 2 rows Rib 42, yf, sl 1, yb, turn, sl 1, rib to end.

Rib a further 29 rows across all sts. Cast off in rib.

COLLAR

With 3¼mm (No 10/US 3) needles cast on 186 sts. Work 30 rows in rib as given for Back. Cast off in rib.

BELT

With 3¼mm (No 10/US 3) needles cast on 14 sts.

Work in rib as given for Back until Belt measures approximately 140(150: 160)cm/55(59:63)in. Cast off in rib.

TO MAKE UP

Catch down pocket linings and sides of pocket tops. Join shoulder seams. Pin cast on edge of collar along row ends of front collars, remainder of front neck edges and along back neck, sew in place. Sew on sleeves, placing centre of sleeves to shoulder seams. Join side and sleeve seams, reversing seam on cuffs. Turn back cuffs. With crochet hook, make loops at side seams in desired position for belt.

TUNIC

BACK
Work as given for Back of Jacket but working 4cm/1½in in rib instead of 10cm/4in.

FRONT
Work as given for Back until Front measures 40(43:46)cm/15¾(17:18)in, from beg, ending with a right side row.

Shape Neck

Next row Patt 66(75:85), cast off next 27(28:27) sts, patt to end.

Work on last set of 66(75:85) sts. Dec one st at neck edge on 4th row and every foll 8th(8th:7th) row until 56(65:73) sts rem. Patt 9(9:4) rows. Mark last row at neck edge. Cont straight until Front matches Back to shoulder shaping, ending at side edge.

Shape Shoulder

Cast off 28(32:36) sts at beg of next row. Work 1 row. Cast off rem 28(33:37) sts.

With right side facing, rejoin yarn to rem sts and patt to end. Complete as first side.

SLEEVES
Work as Sleeves of Jacket.

RIGHT FRONT COLLAR
With 3¼mm (No 10/US 3) needles and right side facing, k up 62 sts along right front neck to marker. Complete as Right Front Band and Collar of Jacket.

LEFT FRONT COLLAR
With 3¼mm (No 10/US 3) needles, right side facing and beg at marker, k up 62 sts down left front neck. Complete as Left Front Band and Collar of Jacket.

COLLAR
Work as Collar of Jacket.

TO MAKE UP
Lap front collars over and catch down row ends to centre of front neck. Join shoulder seams. Pin cast on edge of collar along top row ends of front collars, remainder of front neck edges and along back neck, sew in place. Sew on sleeves, placing centre of sleeves to shoulder seams. Join side and sleeve seams, reversing seams on cuffs. Turn back cuffs.

Susie in the Cable and Moss Stitch Tunic with baby Cairo in the Boxy Moss Stitch Jacket (see page 44).

BOXY MOSS STITCH JACKET

This design is so simple it is perfect for beginners, or for knitters who are looking for something easy and quick. Worked in moss stitch with turned-back cuffs and pockets, it is edged in blanket stitch.

MEASUREMENTS

To fit ages/sizes	1yr	1-2yrs	2-3yrs	3-4yrs	4-6yrs	6-8yrs	8-10yrs	10-12yrs	small	medium	large
Actual chest/bust	64	70	77	81	86	90	96	100	104	108	112 cm
measurement	25¼	27½	30¼	32	34	35½	37¾	39½	41	42½	44 in
Length	30	33	35	37	39	42	44	46	48	50	52 cm
	12	13	13¾	14½	15½	16½	17¼	18	19	19¾	20½ in
Sleeve seam	21	24	27	30	33	36	39	43	46	48	50 cm
	8¼	9½	10¾	11¾	13	14	15¼	17	18¼	19	19¾ in

MATERIALS
6(7:8:9:10:12:13:14:15:16:17) 50g balls of Rowan DK Tweed in main colour (A).
Small amount of same in contrast colour (B) for embroidery.
Pair each of 3¼mm (No 10/US 3) and 4mm (No 8/US 6) knitting needles.
4(5:5:5:5:6:6:6:7:7:7) buttons.

TENSION
21 sts and 36 rows to 10cm/4in square over moss st on 4mm (No 8/US 6) needles.

ABBREVIATIONS
See page 7.

BACK
With 4mm (No 8/US 6) needles and A, cast on 67(73: 81: 85: 91:95:101:105: 109:113:117) sts.
1st row K1, [p1, k1] to end.
This row forms moss st. Cont in moss st until Back measures 30(33:35:37:39: 42:44:46:48:50:52)cm/12(13:13¾:14½: 15½:16½:17¼:18:19:19¾:20½)in from beg.
Shape Shoulders
Cast off 10(11:13:13:14:15:16:16:17:17: 18) sts at beg of next 2 rows and 11(12:13:14:15: 15:16:17:17:18:18) sts at beg of foll 2 rows. Cast off rem 25(27:29:31:33:35: 37:39:41:43:45) sts.

POCKET LININGS (MAKE 2)
With 4mm (No 8/US 6) needles and A, cast on 17(19:19:21:21:23:23:25:27: 27:27) sts. Work 7(8:8:9:9:10:10:11:12: 12:12)cm/2¾(3¼:3¼:3½:3½:4:4:4¼:4¾:4¾: 4¾)in in moss st. Leave these sts on a spare needle.

LEFT FRONT FOR GIRLS, **RIGHT FRONT** FOR BOYS
With 4mm (No 8/US 6) needles and A, cast on 35(39:43:45:49:51:53:55:57: 61:63) sts.
Work in moss st until Front measures 9(10:10:11:11:12:12:13:14:14:14)cm/3½ (4:4:4¼:4¼:4¾:4¾:5:5½:5½:5½)in from beg, ending at side edge.
Place Pocket
Next row Moss st 8(10:12:12:14:14: 14:14:14:16:18), cast off next 17(19:19: 21:21:23:23:25:27:27:27) sts, moss st to end.
Next row Moss st 10(10:12:12:14:14: 16:16:16:18:18), moss st across sts of pocket lining, moss st to end.
Cont in moss st across all sts until Front measures 20(22:23:24:25:27:28: 29:30:31:32)cm/8(8¾:9:9½:10:10½:11: 11½:12:12¼:12½)in from beg, ending at side edge.
Shape Neck
Dec one st at neck edge on next row, 10 foll alt rows, then on every 2nd (2nd:2nd:2nd:2nd:2nd:3rd:3rd:3rd:3rd: 3rd) row until 21(23:26:27:29:30:32:33: 34:35:36) sts rem. Cont straight until Front matches Back to shoulder shaping, ending at side edge.
Shape Shoulder
Cast off 10 (11:13:13:14:15:16:16:17: 17:18) sts at beg of next row. Work 1 row. Cast off rem 11(12:13:14:15:15:16: 17:17:18:18) sts.
Mark front edge to indicate buttons: first one 1cm/¼in up from lower edge, last one 2cm/¾in below neck shaping and rem 2(3:3:3:3:4:4:4:5:5:5) evenly spaced between.

Boxy Moss Stitch Jacket (left), Cable and Moss Stitch Tunic (centre; see page 43), and Fairisle Sweater (right; see page 19).

RIGHT FRONT FOR GIRLS,
LEFT FRONT FOR BOYS

With 4mm (No 8/US 6) needles and A, cast on 35(39:43:45:49:51:53:55:57:61:63) sts.

Work in moss st for 1cm/¼in, ending at front edge.

Buttonhole row Moss st 3, yf, k2 tog, moss st to end.

Complete as given for Left Front for girls or Right Front for boys, making buttonholes to match markers and placing pocket as follows:

Next row Moss st 10(10:12:12:14:14:16:16:16:18:18), cast off next 17(19:19:21:21:23:23:25:27:27:27) sts, moss st to end.

Next row Moss st 8(10:12:12:14:14:14:14:14:16:18), moss st across sts of pocket lining, moss st to end.

SLEEVES

With 4mm (No 8/US 6) needles and A cast on 33(35:37:39:43:47:49:51:53:57:59) sts. Work in moss st for 3(4:4:5:5:6:6:7:8:8:8)cm/1¼(1½:1½:2:2:2¼:2¼:2¾:3:3:3)in.

Change to 3¼mm (No 10/US 3) needles.

Work in moss st for a further 3(4:4:5:5:6:6:7:8:8:8)cm/1¼(1½:1½:2:2:2¼:2¼:2¾:3:3:3)in.

Change to 4mm (No 8/US 6) needles. Cont in moss st, inc one st at each end of next row and every foll 5th(4th:4th:4th:4th:5th:5th:5th:5th:5th:6th) row until there are 55(61:67:73:79:83:87:91:95:99:101) sts. Cont straight until Sleeve measures 24(28:31:35:38:42:45:50:54:56:58)cm/9½(11:12¼:13¾:15:16½:17¾:19¾:21¼:22:22¾)in from beg. Cast off.

TO MAKE UP

Join shoulder seams. Sew on sleeves, placing centre of sleeves to shoulder seams. Beginning 3(3:4:4:4:5:5:5:6:6:6)cm/1¼(1¼:1½:1½:1½:2:2:2:2¼:2¼:2¼)in up from lower edges, join side seams then sleeve seams, reversing seams on cuffs. Catch down pocket linings. Sew on buttons. With B, work blanket stitch around lower edges of sleeves, along pocket tops and along lower edge (including side openings), front edges and around neck edge of Jacket. Turn back cuffs.

Simple sweater with polo neck or shawl collar

This easy, stocking stitch sweater is knitted in a soft, chunky-weight yarn and is quick to knit. The polo neck, pictured on page 48, is worn by my son Billy and his friends Cabral and Ibrahim.

MEASUREMENTS

To fit ages/sizes	2-4yrs	4-6yrs	6-8yrs	8-10yrs	10-12yrs	small	medium	large	extra large
Actual chest/bust measurement	82	91	97	106	114	122	128	131	136 cm
	32¼	36	38	41¾	45	48	50½	51½	53½ in
Length	43	48	52	56	62	66	68	70	72 cm
	17	19	20½	22	24½	26	26¾	27½	28¼ in
Sleeve seam	28	32	36	40	44	46	48	50	52 cm
	11	12½	14	15¾	17¼	18	19	19¾	20½ in

MATERIALS
5(6:6:7:8:9:10:11:12) 100g balls of Rowan Chunky for each sweater.
Pair each of 5½mm (No 5/US 9) and 6½mm (No 3/US 10½) knitting needles.
One 6½mm (No 3/US 10½) circular needle for shawl collar jacket.

TENSION
14 sts and 20 rows to 10cm/4in square over st st on 6½mm (No 3/US 10½) needles.

ABBREVIATIONS
See page 7.

POLO NECK SWEATER

BACK
With 5½mm (No 5/US 9) needles, cast on 58(62:66:74:78:86:90:90:94) sts.
1st rib row (right side) K2, [p2, k2] to end.
2nd rib rowP2, [k2, p2] to end.
These 2 rows form rib. Rep them 2(2:2:3:3:3:4:4:4) times more, inc 0(2:2:0:2:0:0:2:2) sts evenly on last row.

58(64:68:74:80:86:90:92:96) sts.
Change to 6½mm (No 3/US 10½) needles.
Beg with a k row, work in st st until Back measures 43(48:52:56:62:66:68:70:72)cm/17(19:20½:22:24½:26:26¾:27½:28¼) in from beg, ending with a p row.

Shape Shoulders
Cast off 10(11:12:13:14:15:15:15:16) sts at beg of next 2 rows and 10(12:12:13:14:15:16:16:16) sts at beg of foll 2 rows. Leave rem 18(18:20:22:24:26:28:30:32) sts on a holder.

FRONT
Work as given for Back until Front measures 39(43:47:51:56:60:62:63:65)cm/15½(17:18½:20:22:23½:24¼:24¾:25½)in from beg, ending with a p row.

Shape Neck
Next row K24(27:28:31:33:36:38:38:39), turn.
Work on this set of sts only. Dec one st at neck edge on every row until 20(23:24:26:28:30:31:31:32) sts rem. Cont straight until Front matches Back to shoulder shaping, ending at side edge.

Shape Shoulder
Cast off 10(11:12:13:14:15:15:15:16) sts at beg of next row. Work 1 row. Cast off rem 10(12:12:13:14:15:16:16:16) sts.
With right side facing, slip centre 10(10:12:12:14:14:14:16:18) sts onto a holder, rejoin yarn to rem sts and k to end.
Complete as first side.

SLEEVES
With 5½mm (No 5/US 9) needles cast on 22(26:26:30:30:34:38:42:42) sts.
Work 10(10:10:12:12:12:16:16:16) rows in rib as given for Back, inc 2(0:2:0:4:2:2:0:4) sts evenly on last row. 24(26:28:30:34:36:40:42:46) sts.
Change to 6½mm (No 3/US 10½) needles.
Beg with a k row, work in st st, inc one st at each end of 5th row and every foll 3rd(3rd:4th:4th:5th:5th:5th:6th:6th) row until there are 48(50:54:56:60:62:66:68:72) sts. Cont straight until Sleeve measures 28(32:36:40:44:46:48:50:52)cm/11(12½:14:15¾:17¼:18:19:19¾:20½)in from beg, ending with a wrong side row. Cast off.

POLO NECK
Join right shoulder seam.
With 5½mm (No 5/US 9) needles and right side facing, k up 11(13:13:14:14:15:16:16:16) sts down left front neck, k centre front sts, k up 11(13:13:14:14:15:16:16:16) sts up right front neck, k back

neck sts. 50(54:58:62:66:70:74:78:82) sts. Work 28(32:32:36:36:40:40:40:40) rows in rib as given for Back. Cast off loosely in rib.

TO MAKE UP

Join left shoulder and polo neck seam, reversing seam half way on polo neck. Sew on sleeves, placing centre of sleeves to shoulder seams. Join side and sleeve seams.

SHAWL COLLAR SWEATER

BACK

Work as given for Back of Polo Neck Sweater, but cast off back neck sts.

FRONT

Work as given for Back until Front measures 27(31:34:37:41:44:45:46:47)cm/10½(12¼:13½:14½:16¼:17¼:17¾:18:18½)in from beg, ending with a k row.

Shape Neck

Next row P20(23:24:26:28:30:31:31:32), cast off next 18(18:20:22:24:26:28:30:32) sts, p to end.

Work straight on last set of sts only until Front matches Back to shoulder shaping, ending at side edge.

Shape Shoulder

Cast off 10(11:12:13:14:15:15:15:16) sts at beg of next row. Work 1 row. Cast off rem 10(12:12:13:14:15:16:16:16) sts.

With right side facing, rejoin yarn to rem sts and complete as first side.

SLEEVES

Work as Sleeves of Polo Neck Sweater.

COLLAR

Join shoulder seams.

With 6½mm (No 3/US 10½) circular needle and right side facing, k up 32(34:35:38:42:45:46:49:50) sts along straight right front neck edge, 22(22:24:26:30:32:34:36:38) sts across back neck and 32(34:35:38:42:45:46: 49:50) sts along straight left front neck edge. 86(90:94:102:114:122:126:134: 138) sts.

Work backwards and forwards.

1st rib row P2, [k2, p2] to end.

2nd rib row K2, [p2, k2] to end.

Rep last 2 rows until collar measures 13(13:14:16:17:18:20:21:23)cm/5(5:5½:6¼:6¾:7:8:8¼:9)in. Cast off loosely in rib.

TO MAKE UP

Lap row ends edges of collar over and catch down to cast off sts at base of front neck. Sew on sleeves, placing centre of sleeves to shoulder seams. Join side and sleeve seams.

The Simple Sweater with Shawl collar

SNOWFLAKE AND HEART JACKET WITH ZIP

This design is based on a 1950s college-style jacket and has embroidered cross stitch detailing with moss stitch patterning and borders. It has pockets, a neat shawl collar and is knitted in a pure wool Aran-weight yarn for a crisp finish.

MATERIALS
6(7:8:9:9:10) 100g hanks of Rowan Magpie in Black (A).
1 hank of same in Cream.
1 50g ball of Rowan Designer DK Wool in Red.
Pair each of 3¾mm (No 9/US 4), 4mm (No 8/US 6) and 4½mm (No 7/US 7) knitting needles.
40(45:45:50:55:55)cm/16(18:18:20:22:22)in open-ended zip fastener.

MEASUREMENTS

To fit ages/sizes	4-6yrs	6-8yrs	8-10yrs	small	medium	large
Actual chest/bust	92	96	101	110	114	119 cm
measurement	36¼	38	39¾	43¼	45	47 in
Length	46	49	52	55	60	62 cm
	18	19¼	20½	21¾	23½	24½ in
Sleeve seam	33	36	40	46	48	48 cm
	13	14	15¾	18	19	19 in

TENSION
18 sts and 26 rows to 10cm/4in square over st st on 4½mm (No 7/US 7) needles.

ABBREVIATIONS
See page 7.

NOTES
Read charts from right to left on right side (k) rows and from left to right on wrong side (p) rows. Use separate lengths of contrast colours when working heart or snowflake motifs and twist yarns together on wrong side at joins to avoid holes.

BACK
With 3¾mm (No 9/US 4) needles and A, cast on 83(87:91:99:103:107) sts.
Work welt patt as follows:
1st row K1, [p1, k1] to end.
This row forms moss st. Moss st 4 more rows.

Snowflake and Heart Jacket with Zip (right) and Scandinavian Jacket (left; see page 62).

6th row (right side) [K1, p1] 0(1:0:0:1:0) time, k3, [p1, k1, p1, k1, p1, k3] to last 0(2:0:0:2:0) sts, [p1, k1] 0(1:0:0:1:0) time.
7th row P4(0:4:4:0:4), k1, [p1, k1] 1(0:1:1:0:1) time, [p5, k1, p1, k1] to last 4(6:4:4:6:4) sts, p4(5:4:4:5:4), k0(1:0:0:1:0).
8th row K5(7:5:5:7:5), [p1, k7] to last 6(8:6:6:8:6) sts, p1, k to end.
Change to 4½mm (No 7/US 7) needles.
Beg with a p row, work 3 rows in st st. Stranding yarn not in use loosely across wrong side, work the 3 rows of chart 1.
Cont in A only until Back measures 29 (32:34:37:42:43)cm/11¼(12½:13½:14½:16½:17)in from beg, ending with a wrong side row. Work the 3 rows of chart 1. With A, st st 3 rows.
Next row K4(4:6:7:7:9)A, *k 1st row of chart 2, k3(4:4:5:6:6)A, k 1st row of chart 3, k3(4:4:5:6:6)A, k 1st row of chart 2*; k5(5:5:7:7:7)A, rep from * to *, with A, k to end.
Next row P4(4:6:7:7:9)A, * p 2nd row of chart 2, p3(4:4:5:6:6)A, p 2nd row of chart 3, p3(4:4:5:6:6)A, p 2nd row of chart 2*; p5(5:5:7:7:7)A, rep from * to *, with A, p to end.
Work a further 9 rows as set. With A, st st 3 rows, then work the 3 rows of chart 1. Cont in A only, st st 3 rows, then work 8th, 7th and 6th rows of welt patt. Cont in moss st across all sts until Back measures 46(49:52:55:60:62)cm/18(19¼:20½:21¾:23½:24½)in from beg, ending with a right side row.
Shape Shoulders and Neck
Next row Moss st 33(34:35:38:39:40), cast off next 17(19:21:23:25:27) sts, moss st to end.
Work on last set of sts only. Cast off 15(16:16:18:18:19) sts at beg of next row and 3 sts at beg of foll row. Cast off rem 15(15:16:17:18:18) sts.
With right side facing, rejoin yarn to rem sts and moss st to end. Complete as first side.

POCKET LININGS (MAKE 2)
With 4½mm (No 7/US 7) needles and A, cast on 21(21:23:23:25:25) sts. Beg with a k row, work 27(27:29:29:33:33) rows in st st. Leave these sts on a holder.

Star and Heart Sweater

A patchwork of textured hearts and stars, this generous sweater has moss stitch sleeves and a moss stitch, rolled over collar.

MATERIALS

12 100g hanks of Rowan Magpie.
Pair of 4½mm (No 7/US 7) knitting needles.

MEASUREMENTS

To fit bust	86-102cm 34-40in
Actual bust measurement	120cm 47¼in
Length	68cm 26¾in
Sleeve seam (with cuff turned back)	46cm 18 in

TENSIONS

18 sts and 26 rows to 10cm/4in square over st st on 4½mm (No 7/US 7) needles.
19 sts and 30 rows to 10cm/4in square over moss st on 4½mm (No 7/US 7) needles.

ABBREVIATIONS

See page 7.

BACK

With 4½mm (No 7/US 7) needles cast on 111 sts.
1st row K1, [p1, k1] to end.
This row forms moss st. Work 11 rows more in moss st.
Work in patt as follows:
1st row (right side) Moss st 12, work 1st row of chart 1, moss st 3, work 1st row of chart 2, moss st 3, work 1st row of chart 1, moss st 12.
2nd to 38th rows Rep last row 37 times, but working 2nd to 38th rows of charts.
39th to 42nd rows K1, [p1, k1] to end.
43rd row Moss st 12, work 1st row of chart 2, moss st 3, work 1st row of chart 1, moss st 3, work 1st row of chart 2, moss st 12.
44th to 80th rows Rep last row 37 times, but working 2nd to 38th rows of charts.
81st to 84th rows K1, [p1, k1] to end.
These 84 rows form patt. Patt a further 80 rows.** Cont in moss st across all st, work 8 rows.
Shape Neck
Next row Patt 42, turn.
Work on this set of sts only. Cast off 3 sts at beg of next row and foll alt row. Cast off rem 36 sts.
With right side facing, slip centre 27 sts onto a holder, rejoin yarn to rem sts, cast off 3, patt to end. Work 1 row. Cast off 3 sts at beg of next row. Work 1 row. Cast off rem 36 sts.

FRONT

Work as given for Back to **.
Continuing in moss st across all sts, work as follows:
Shape Neck
Next row Patt 42, turn.
Work on this set of sts only. Dec one st at neck edge on next 6 rows. 36 sts.
Patt 5 rows straight. Cast off.
With right side facing, slip centre 27 sts onto a holder, rejoin yarn to rem sts and patt to end. Complete as first side.

SLEEVES

With 4½mm (No 7/US 7) needles cast on 49 sts. Work 16 rows in moss st as

Chart 1

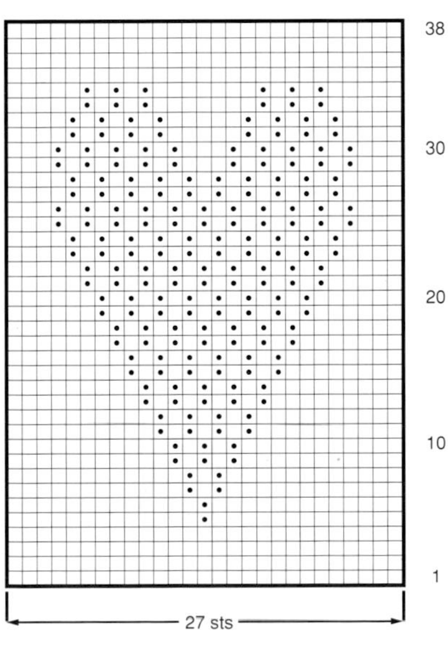

Chart 2

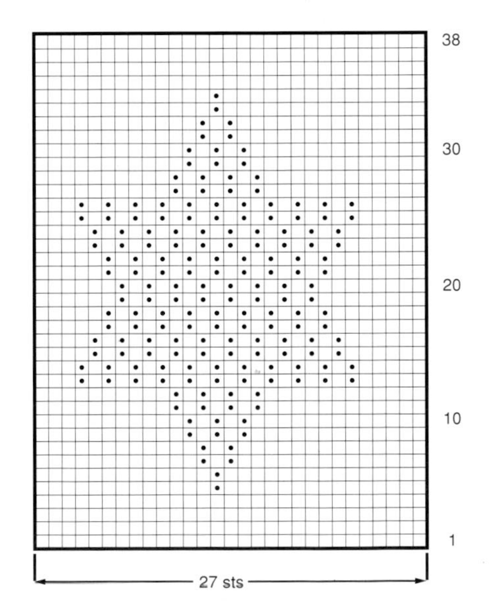

Key

□ = K on right side
P on wrong side

⊡ = P on right side
K on wrong side

given for Back, dec one st at each end of 5th row and foll 6th row. 45 sts. Cont in moss st, inc one st at each end of 9th row and every foll 4th row until there are 91 sts. Cont straight until Sleeve measures 51cm/20in from beg. Cast off.

COLLAR

Join right shoulder seam.
With 4½mm (No 7/US 7) needles and right side facing, k up 13 sts down left front neck, work p1, [k1, p1] 13 times across centre front sts, k up 12 sts up right front neck, 7 sts down right back neck, work p1, [k1, p1] 13 times across centre back sts, k up 7 sts up left back neck. 93 sts.
1st rib row P1, [k1, p1] to end.
2nd rib row K1, [p1, k1] to end.
Rib 12 rows more. Work 20 rows in moss st as given for Back. Cast off firmly.

TO MAKE UP

Join left shoulder and collar seam, reversing seam on moss st section of collar. Sew on sleeves, placing centre of sleeves to shoulder seams. Join side and sleeve seams, reversing seams on first 16 rows at lower edge of sleeves for cuffs. Turn back cuffs.

HEART AND STAR BABY WRAP

Continuing the heart and star theme, the wrap is knitted in a pure wool double-knitting yarn and has cross stitch embroidery. If preferred, the colour motifs can be embroidered on afterwards to give an authentic patchwork quilt effect.

MATERIALS

5 50g balls of Rowan Designer DK Wool in Cream (A).
1 ball of same in Red (B).
Pair of 4mm (No 8/US 6) knitting needles.
Cable needle.

MEASUREMENT

Approximately 53cm x 79cm/21in x 31in.

TENSION

24 sts and 32 rows to 10cm/4in square over st st on 4mm (No 8/US 6) needles.

ABBREVIATIONS

C4B = sl next 2 sts onto cable needle and leave at back of work, k2, then k2 from cable needle.
Also see page 7.

NOTES

Read charts from right to left on right side and from left to right on wrong side. When working colour motifs, use separate small ball of B for each coloured area and twist yarn together on wrong side when changing colour to avoid holes. If desired, the colour motifs can be Swiss darned (see diagrams, page 66) when knitting is complete.

TO MAKE

With 4mm (No 8/US 6) needles and A, cast on 129 sts.
1st row (right side) P1, k1, p1, k4, p1, [k1, p1] to last 7 sts, k4, p1, k1, p1.
2nd row P1, k1, p6, k1, [p1, k1] to last 8 sts, p6, k1, p1.
3rd row P1, k1, p1, C4B, p1, [k1, p1] to last 7 sts, C4B, p1, k1, p1.
4th row As 2nd row.
These 4 rows form moss st with cable patt at side edges. Work 2 more rows.
7th row Patt 10, work 1st row of chart 1, moss st 3, work 1st row of chart 2, moss st 3, work 1st row of chart 3, moss st 3, work 1st row of chart 4, patt 10.
8th row Patt 10, work 2nd row of chart 4, moss st 3, work 2nd row of chart 3, moss st 3, work 2nd row of chart 2, moss st 3, work 2nd row of chart 1, patt 10.
9th to 44th rows Rep last 2 rows 18 times more but working 3rd to 38th rows of charts.
45th row Patt 8, moss st to last 8 sts, patt 8.
46th to 48th rows Rep last row 3 times.
49th row Patt 10, work 1st row of chart 4, moss st 3, work 1st row of chart 1, moss st 3, work 1st row of chart 2, moss st 3, work 1st row of

chart 3, patt 10.
50th row Patt 10, work 2nd row of chart 3, moss st 3, work 2nd row of chart 2, moss st 3, work 2nd row of chart 1, moss st 3, work 2nd row of chart 4, patt 10.
51st to 90th rows Work 9th to 48th rows.
91st row Patt 10, work 1st row of chart 3, moss st 3, work 1st row of chart 4, moss st 3, work 1st row of chart 1, moss st 3, work 1st row of chart 2, patt 10.
92nd row Patt 10, work 2nd row of chart 2, moss st 3, work 2nd row of chart 1, moss st 3, work 2nd row of chart 4, moss st 3, work 2nd row of chart 3, patt 10.
93rd to 132nd rows Work 9th to 48th rows.
133rd row Patt 10, work 1st row of chart 2, moss st 3, work 1st row of chart 3, moss st 3, work 1st row of chart 4, moss st 3, work 1st row of chart 1, patt 10.
134th row Patt 10, work 2nd row of chart 1, moss st 3, work 2nd row of chart 4, moss st 3, work 2nd row of chart 3, moss st 3, work 2nd row of chart 2, patt 10.
135th to 174th rows Work 9th to 48th rows.
175th to 258th rows Work 7th to 90th rows.
259th and 260th rows Rep 45th row twice.
Cast off in patt, working 2 sts tog twice over each cable. Embroider single cross stitch in B on moss st along lower and top edges and along inside moss st panels at side edges. With B, make 4 pom-poms and attach firmly to each corner.

Overleaf: (left) Heart and Star Baby Wrap; (right) Scandinavian Jacket (right; see page 62) and Star and Heart Sweater (left; see page 57).

Chart 1

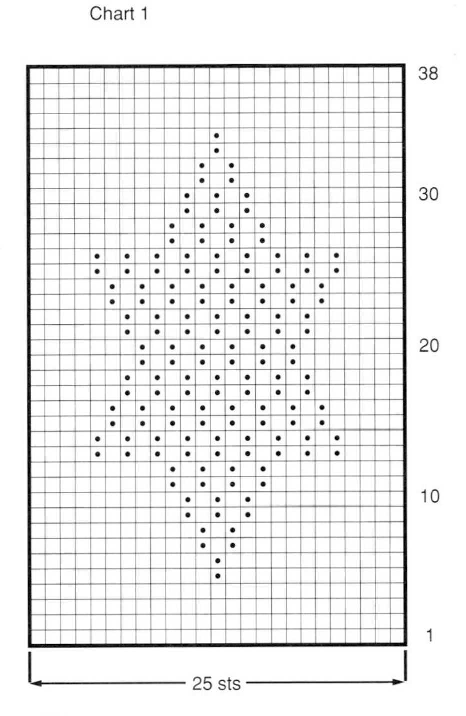

Chart 2

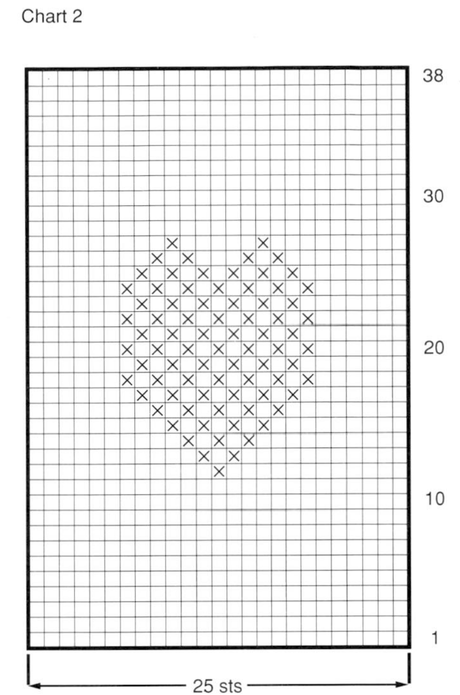

Key

☐ = With A, K on right side, P on wrong side

⊡ = With A, P on right side, K on wrong side

☒ = With B, K on right side, P on wrong side

Chart 3

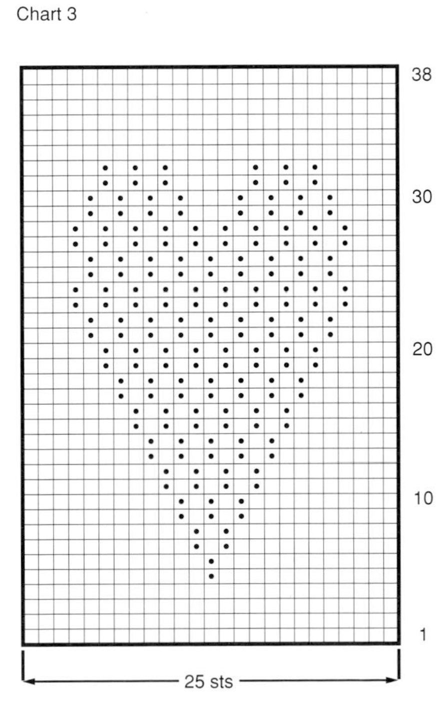

Chart 4

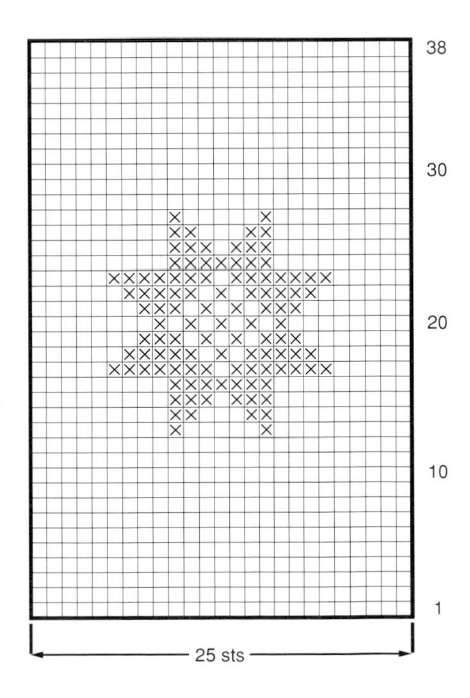

SCANDINAVIAN JACKET

Hearts and snowflakes are featured in this red and cream jacket, which uses traditional Scandinavian patterning. Cross stitch embroidery adds to a folkloric look, and this design has patch pockets.

MATERIALS
4(5:7:9:10) 50g balls of Rowan Designer DK Wool in Red (A).
1(1:1:2:2) balls of same in Cream.
Pair each of 3¼mm (No 10/US 3) and 4mm (No 8/US 6) knitting needles.
5(5:6:6:7) buttons.

TENSION
24 sts and 32 rows to 10cm/4in square over st st on 4mm (No 8/US 6) needles.

ABBREVIATIONS
See page 7.

NOTES
Read charts from right to left on right side (k) rows and from left to right on wrong side (p) rows. When working in pattern, strand yarn not in use loosely across wrong side over no more than 5 sts at the time to keep fabric elastic. Use separate length of Cream when working motif on pockets and twist yarns together on wrong side at joins to avoid holes.

MEASUREMENTS

To fit age	1yr	1-2yrs	3-5yrs	6-8yrs	9-11yrs	
Actual chest	63	73	82	93	102	cm
measurement	24¾	28	32¼	36½	40	in
Length	30	35	40	44	48	cm
	11¾	13¾	15¾	17¼	19	in
Sleeve seam	18	22	26	36	40	cm
	7	8¾	10¼	14	15¾	in

BACK
With 3¼mm (No 10/US 3) needles and A, cast on 73(85:97:109:121) sts.
1st row K1, [p1, k1] to end.
This row forms moss st. Work 7(7:11:13:13) rows more in moss st.
Change to 4mm (No 8/US 6) needles.
Beg with a k row, work 2 rows in st st.
Cont in st st and work 1st, 2nd and 3rd rows of chart 1. With A only, cont in st st until work measures 16(21:26:26:30)cm/6¼(8¼:10¼:10¼:12)in from beg, ending with a p row. Work 36(36:36:50:50) rows of chart 1, beg 2nd rep of patt on 4th and 5th sizes only with 6th row. Cont in A only, work 2 rows.
Shape Shoulders
Cast off 10(12:15:17:20) sts at beg of next 2 rows and 10(13:15:18:20) sts at beg of foll 2 rows. Leave rem 33(35:37:39:41) sts on a holder.

LEFT FRONT
With 3¼mm (No 10/US 3) needles and A, cast on 41(47:53:59:65) sts.
Work 8(8:12:14:14) rows in moss st as given for Back, inc one st at centre of last row. 42(48:54:60:66) sts.
Change to 4mm (No 8/US 6) needles.
1st row (right side) K to last 5 sts, moss st 5.
2nd row Moss st 5, p to end.
Keeping the 5 sts at front edge in moss st and A and remainder in st st, work 1st, 2nd and 3rd rows of chart 1. With A only, cont in st st with 5 sts at front edge in moss st until Front measures 16(21:26:26:30)cm/6¼(8¼:10¼:10¼:12)in from beg, ending with a wrong side row. Working in st st with 5 sts at front edge in moss st and A, patt 25(25:23:35:35) rows from chart 1.
Shape neck
Next row With A, moss st 5 and slip these 5 sts onto safety pin, patt to end.
Patt 1 row. Keeping patt correct, cast off 5(6:6:6:6) sts at beg of next row and 6 sts at beg of foll alt row. Dec one st at neck edge on every row until 20(25:30:35:40) sts rem. Patt 0(0:1:2:1) rows. Cont in A only, work 2 rows.
Shape Shoulder
Cast off 10(12:15:17:20) sts at beg of next row. Work 1 row. Cast off rem 10(13:15:18:20) sts.
Mark front edge to indicate buttons: first one on 5th row of welt and last one on last row before neck shaping and rem 3(3:4:4:5) evenly spaced between.

RIGHT FRONT
With 3¼mm (No 10/US 3) needles and A, cast on 41(47:53:59:65) sts.
Work 4 rows in moss st as given for Back.
Buttonhole row (right side) K1, p1, k2 tog, yf, k1, patt to end.
Moss st 3(3:7:9:9) rows more, inc one st at centre of last row. 42(48:54:60:66) sts.
Change to 4mm (No 8/US 6) needles.
1st row (right side) Moss st 5, k to end.
2nd row P to last 5 sts, moss st 5.
Complete to match Left Front, making buttonholes to match markers as before.

SLEEVES

With 3¼mm (No 10/US 3) needles and A, cast on 33(37:41:45:49) sts.
Work 12(12:16:18:18) rows in moss st as given for Back, inc 10 sts evenly across last row. 43(47:51:55:59) sts.
Change to 4mm (No 8/US 6) needles.
Beg with a k row, work 2 rows in st st.
Cont in st st, work first 3 rows of chart 1, then cont in A only, **at the same time**, inc one st at each end of 1st row and every foll 2nd(3rd:4th:5th:6th) row until there are 67(71:75:79:83) sts.
Work 1(2:1:4:5) rows straight. Beg with 15th(15th:15th:1st:1st) row, work 22(22:22:38:38) rows of chart 1, inc and work into patt one st at each end of 1st(1st:3rd:1st:1st) row and 1(2:4:4:5) foll 2nd(3rd:4th:5th:6th) rows. 71(77:85:89:95) sts. Cast off.

NECKBAND

Join shoulder seams.
With 3¼mm (No 10/US 3) needles and right side facing, slip the 5 sts from right front safety pin onto needle, rejoin A yarn and k up 19(21:23:25:27) sts up right front neck, k centre back sts, k up 19(21:23:25:27) sts down left front neck, then moss st 5 sts from left front safety pin. 81(87:93:99:105) sts.
Moss st 6(6:6:8:8) rows. Cast off in moss st.

POCKETS (MAKE 2)

With 4mm (No 8/US 6) needles and A, cast on 21(23:23:25:27) sts.
Work 4 rows in moss st.
Next row Moss st 4, k to last 4 sts, moss st 4.
Next row Moss st 4, p to last 4 sts, moss st 4.
Rep last 2 rows 0(1:2:2:2) times more.
Next row With A, moss st 4, k2(3:3:4:5), k 1st row of chart 2, with A, k2(3:3:4:5), moss st 4.
Next row With A, moss st 4, p2(3:3:4:5), p 2nd row of chart 2, with A, p2(3:3:4:5), moss st 4.
Work a further 7 rows as set. Keeping the 4 sts at each side in moss st and remainder in st st, cont in A only, work 1(3:5:5:5) rows. Moss st 4 rows across all sts. Cast off in moss st.

TO MAKE UP

Sew on sleeves, placing centre of sleeves to shoulder seams. Join side and sleeve seams. Sew on buttons and pockets. With Cream, embroider single cross stitches on moss st hems, cuffs, front bands and neckband. Work single cross stitch with Cream in each corner on pockets.

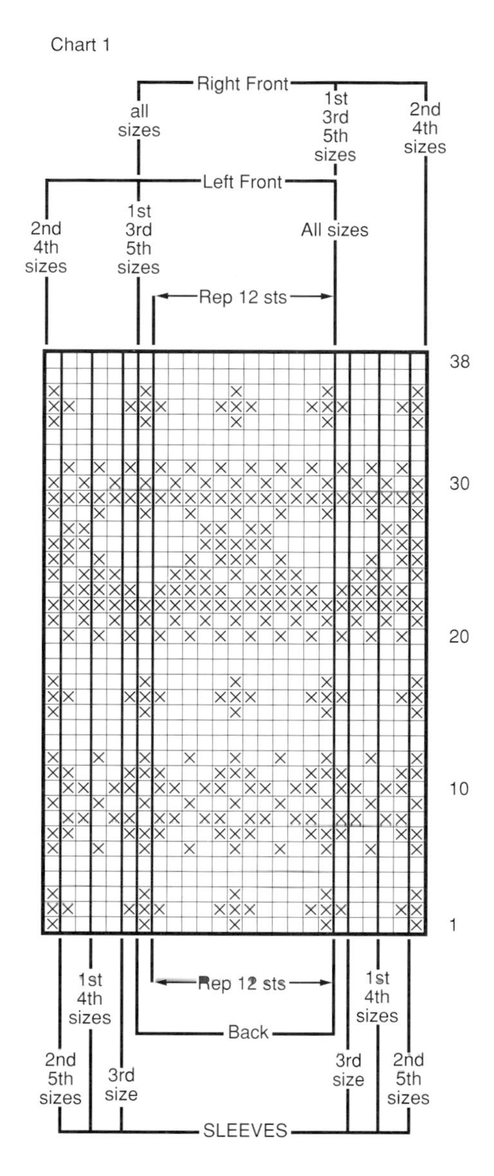

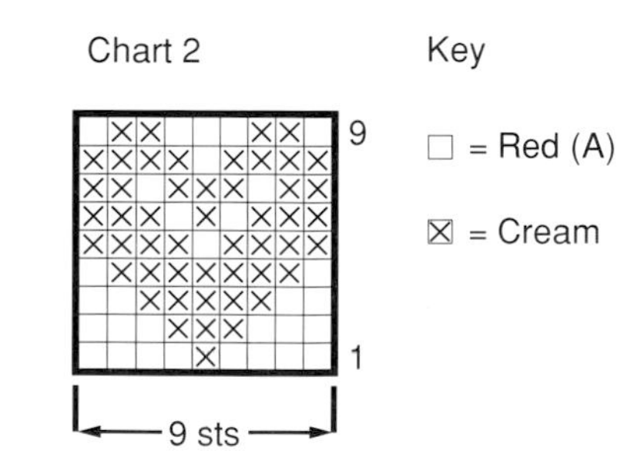

Left Front.
Next row (right side) Moss st 4, k to end.
Next row P to last 4 sts, moss st 4.
Rep last 2 rows until Front measures 7(9:11:14)cm/2¾(3½:4¼5½)in from beg, ending with a wrong side row.
Buttonhole row K1, p1, yrn, p2 tog, patt to end.
Complete as given for Left Front, making buttonholes at markers, reversing shapings and working dec row and patt as follows:
Dec row P8(10:12:14), [p2 tog, p1] 3 times, [p2 tog] twice, * p3 tog, [p2 tog] twice; rep from * 3 times more, p2 tog, [p1, p2 tog] 3 times, p3(5:7:9), moss st 4. 42(46:50:54) sts.
1st row (right side) Moss st 4, k3(5:7:9), p1, C4B, p2, [k1, p1] 7 times, p1, C4F, p1, k8(10:12:14).
2nd row P8(10:12:14), k1, p4, k1, work 1st row of chart 1, k1, p4, k1, p3(5:7:9), moss st 4.
3rd row Moss st 4, k3(5:7:9), p1, k4, p1, work 2nd row of chart 1, p1, k4, p1, k8(10:12:14).
4th row P8(10:12:14), k1, p4, k1, work 3rd row of chart 1, k1, p4, k1, p3(5:7:9), moss st 4.

BACK

With 3¼mm (No 10/US 3) needles and A, cast on 113(121:125:129) sts.
Work 6 rows in moss st as given for Left Front.
Beg with a k row, work in st st until Back matches Left Front to armhole shaping, ending with a p row.

Shape Armholes

Cast off 4 sts at beg of next 2 rows.
Dec one st at each end of next 3 rows. 99(107:111:115) sts. Work 1 row.
Dec row K7(11:13:15), [k 2 tog] to last 8(12:14:16)sts, k to end. 57(65:69:73) sts.
1st row P7(11:13:15), k1, [p1, k1] 21 times, p to end.
2nd row K8(12:14:16), p1, [k1, p1] 20 times, k to end.
3rd row As 1st row.
4th row K7(11:13:15), work 1st row of chart 1 over next 43 sts, k to end.
5th row P7(11:13:15), work 2nd row of chart 1 over next 43 sts, p to end.
6th to 17th rows Rep 4th and 5th rows 6 times but working 3rd to 14th rows of chart.
18th row As 2nd row.
19th and 20th rows As 1st and 2nd rows.
Beg with a p row, cont in st st until Back matches Left Front to shoulder shaping, ending with a p row.

Shape Shoulders

Cast off 6(7:7:7) sts at beg of next 4 rows and 5(6:6:7) sts at beg of foll 2 rows. Cast off rem 23(25:29:31) sts.

SLEEVES

With 3¼mm (No 10/US 3) needles and A, cast on 37(41:43:47) sts.
Work 5 rows in moss st as given for Left Front.
Next row Moss st 1(3:4:3), work twice in next st, [moss st 2, work twice in next st] 11(11:11:13) times, moss st 2(4:5:4). 49(53:55:61) sts.
Beg with a k row, work in st st, inc one st at each end of 9th row and every foll 5th(4th:4th:6th) row until there are 67(73:79:81) sts. Cont straight until Sleeve measures 18(20:22:24)cm/7(8:8¾:9½)in from beg, ending with a p row.

Shape Top

Cast off 4 sts at beg of next 2 rows.
Dec one st at each end of next row and foll alt row. Work 1 row. Cast off rem 55(61:67:69) sts.

COLLAR

Join shoulder seams.
With 3¼mm (No 10/US 3) needles, right side facing, A and beg at centre of buttonhole band, k up 22(22: 25:27) sts up right front neck, 27(27: 29:29) sts across back neck and 22(22: 25:27) sts down left front neck to centre of button band. 71(71:79:83) sts.
Next row K1, [p1, k1] to end.
Rep this row 5 times more.
Change to 3¾mm (No 9/US 4) needles.
Next row Moss st 0(0:4:6) work 1st row of chart 1 over next 71 sts, moss st 0(0:4:6).
Work a further 13 rows as set.
Work 4 rows in moss st across all sts.
Cast off loosely in moss st.

TO MAKE UP

Swiss darn (see diagrams below) flower motif on first and every alternate stocking stitch diamond formed by chart pattern. Join side and sleeve seams. Sew in sleeves. Sew on buttons.

Swiss darning

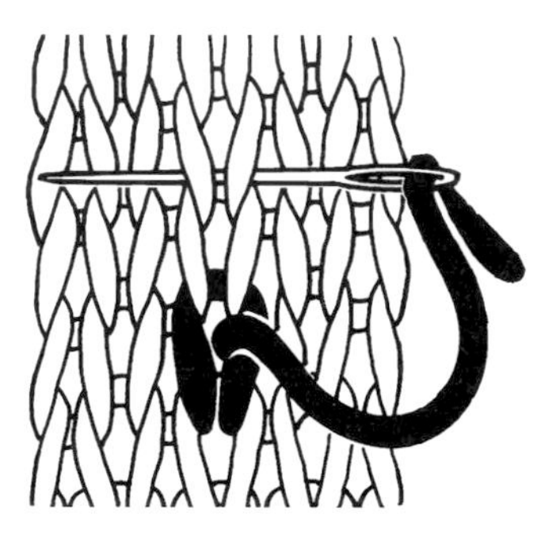

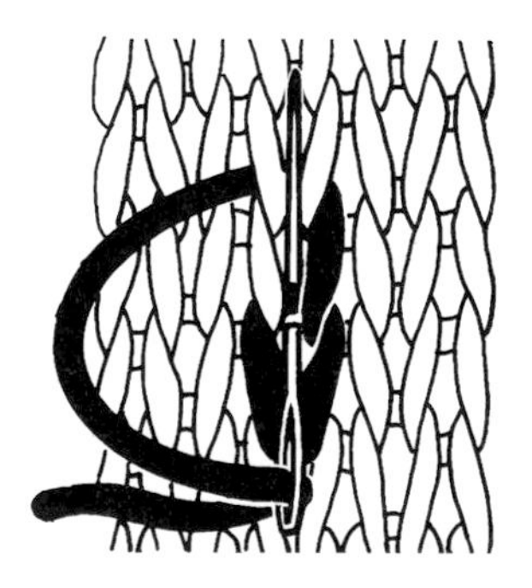

Flower motif

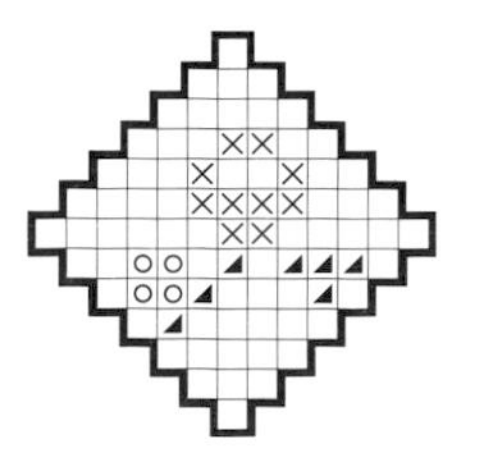

Key

◪ = Green
⊡ = Pale Pink
☒ = Deep Pink

Chenille Jacket

Knitted in a velvety, chunky chenille, this jacket is shaped to give a flattering silhouette but has a small vent at the back for ease over the hips. There is garter stitch detailing in the borders and collar.

MATERIALS
8(8:9) 100g balls of Rowan Chenille Chunky Cotton.
Pair each of 4mm (No 8/US 6) and 4½mm (No 7/US 7) knitting needles.
4 buttons.

MEASUREMENTS

To fit bust	86	91	96 cm
	34	36	38 in
Actual bust measurement	100	105	110 cm
	39¼	41¼	43¼ in
Length	60	61	62 cm
	23½	24	24½ in
Sleeve seam	46	46	46 cm
	18	18	18 in

TENSION
16 sts and 24 rows to 10cm/4in square over st st on 4½mm (No 7/US 7) needles.

ABBREVIATIONS
See page 7.

RIGHT BACK
With 4mm (No 8/US 6) needles cast on 46(48:50) sts.
K 7 rows.
Change to 4½mm (No 7/US 7) needles.
1st row (right side) K.
2nd row K4, p to end.
3rd to 6th rows Rep 1st and 2nd rows twice.
7th row K3, skpo, k23(24:25), k2 tog, k to end.

Chenille Jacket (right) and Rosebud Crossover Cardigan (left; see page 71)

8th row As 2nd row.
9th to 14th rows Rep 1st and 2nd rows 3 times.
15th row K3, skpo, k21(22:23), k2 tog, k to end.
16th row As 2nd row.
17th to 22nd rows Rep 1st and 2nd rows 3 times.
23rd row K3, skpo, k19(20:21), k2 tog, k to end.
24th row As 2nd row. **
Next row K to last 4 sts, cast off these 4 sts. 36(38:40) sts.
Leave these sts on a spare needle.

LEFT BACK
With 4mm (No 8/US 6) needles cast on 46(48:50) sts.
K 7 rows.
Change to 4½mm (No 7/US 7) needles.
1st row (right side) K.
2nd row P to last 4 sts, k4.
3rd to 6th rows Rep 1st and 2nd rows twice.
7th row K16(17:18), skpo, k23(24:25), k2 tog, k3.
8th row As 2nd row.
9th to 14th rows Rep 1st and 2nd rows 3 times.
15th row K16(17:18), skpo, k21(22:23), k2 tog, k3.
16th row As 2nd row.
17th to 22nd rows Rep 1st and 2nd rows 3 times.
23rd row K16(17:18), skpo, k19(20:21), k2 tog, k3.
24th row As 2nd row. ***
K 1 row.
Back
Next row P to end then p across sts of right back. 76(80:84) sts.
Beg with a k row, work 4 rows in st st.
Dec row K3, skpo, k17(18:19), k2 tog, k28(30:32), skpo, k17(18:19), k2 tog, k3.
Work 7 rows straight.
Dec row K3, skpo, k15(16:17), k2 tog, k28(30:32), skpo, k15(16:17), k2 tog, k3. 68(72:76) sts.
Work 9 rows straight.
Inc row K3, m1, k to last 3 sts, m1, k3.
Work 5 rows straight. Rep last 6 rows 5 times more. 80(84:88) sts. Work 2 more rows. Back should measure 39cm/15¼in from beg.
Shape Armholes
Cast off 4 sts at beg of next 2 rows.
1st row K1, skpo, k to last 3 sts, k2 tog, k1.
2nd row P.
Rep these 2 rows 3(4:5) times more. 64(66:68) sts. Cont straight until Back measures 60(61:62)cm/23½(24:24½)in from beg, ending with a p row.
Shape Shoulders
Cast off 9 sts at beg of next 4 rows.
Cast off rem 28(30:32) sts.

LEFT FRONT
Work as given for Right Back to **.
25th to 30th rows Rep 1st and 2nd rows 3 times.
31st row K3, skpo, k17(18:19), k2 tog, k to end.
32nd row As 2nd row.
33rd to 38th rows Rep 1st and 2nd rows 3 times.
39th row K3, skpo, k15(16:17), k2 tog, k to end. 36(38:40) sts.
Keeping the 4 sts at front edge in garter st and remainder in st st, work 9 rows straight.
Inc row K3, m1, k to end.
Work 5 rows straight. Rep last 6 rows 5 times more. 42(44:46) sts. Work 2 more rows.

Change to 3¾mm (No 9/US 4) needles.
1st row (right side) K 1st(19th:1st) row of chart to last 4 sts, k4A.
2nd row K4A, p 2nd(20th:2nd) row of chart to end.
Work a further 10(12:18) rows as set.
Shape Neck
Next row Patt to last 6 sts, k2 tog and turn; leave rem 4 sts on a safety pin.
Next row P2 tog, patt to end.
Next row Patt to last 2 sts, k2 tog.
Rep last 2 rows until 16(18:20) sts rem.
Work 14(16:22) rows straight.
Shape Shoulder
Cast off 8(9:10) sts at beg of next row.
Work 1 row. Cast off rem 8(9:10) sts.

RIGHT FRONT

With 3mm (No 11/US 2) needles and A, cast on 64(72:80) sts.
K 9 rows.
Change to 3¾mm (No 9/US 4) needles.
1st row (right side) K4A, k 1st(19th:1st) row of chart to end.
2nd row P 2nd(20th:2nd) row of chart to last 4 sts, k4A.
Work a further 10(12:18) rows as set.
Shape Neck
Next row K4 and sl these 4 sts onto a safety pin, skpo, k to end.
Next row Patt to last 2 sts, p2 tog tbl.
Next row Skpo, patt to end.
Complete as Left Front, working 1 row more before shaping shoulder.

SLEEVES

With 3mm (No 11/US 2) needles and A, cast on 33(37:43) sts.
K 9 rows, inc 3(3:5) sts evenly across last row. 36(40:48) sts..
Change to 3¾mm (No 9/US 4) needles.
Beg with a k row, work in st st and patt from chart, inc one st at each end of 3rd row and every foll 4th row until there are 58(66:72) sts, working inc sts into patt. Cont straight until Sleeve measures 18(22:24)cm/7(8¾:9½)in from beg, ending with a wrong side row.
Cast off.

NECKBAND

Join shoulder seams.
With 3mm (No 11/US 2) needles and right side facing, sl 4 sts from safety pin at right front on to needle, k up 58(66:78) sts up right front neck to shoulder, k back neck sts, k up 58(66:78) sts down left front neck, then k 4 sts from safety pin. 156(176:204) sts. K 5 rows. Cast off.

TIES (MAKE 2)

With 3mm (No 11/US 2) needles and A, cast on 5 sts. Work in garter st (every row k) until tie measures approximately 40(45:50)cm/16(18:20)in. Cast off.

TO MAKE UP

Sew on sleeves, placing centre of sleeves to shoulder seams. Sew one end of ties to row ends of neckband. Leaving an opening at right side seam for tie, join side and sleeve seams.

FLORAL JACKET

A gently shaped cotton jacket in a pattern of moss stitch and florals. It has a neat back vent and a moss stitch shawl collar.

MATERIALS

15 50g balls of Rowan Cotton Glace in Beige (A).
1 ball of same in each of Green, Light Pink and Dark Pink.
Pair each of 3mm (No 11/US 2) and 3¼mm (No 10/US 3) knitting needles.
5 buttons.

MEASUREMENTS

To fit bust	86-91cm	34-36in
Actual bust measurement	102cm	40in
Length	59cm	23¼in
Sleeve seam	45cm	17¾in

TENSION

25 sts and 36 rows to 10cm/4in square over pattern on 3¼mm (No 10/US 3) needles.

ABBREVIATIONS

See page 7.

NOTES

Read chart from right to left on right side rows and from left to right on wrong side rows. When working in pattern from chart, use separate lengths of contrast colours for each coloured area and twist yarns together on wrong side at joins to avoid holes.

RIGHT BACK

With 3mm (No 11/US 2) needles and A, cast on 66 sts.

1st row (right side) [K1, p1] to end.

2nd row [P1, k1] to end.

These 2 rows form moss st. Moss st 6 rows more.

Change to 3¼mm (No 10/US 3) needles.

1st row Work 15th row of chart to last 5 sts, with A, moss st 5.

2nd row With A, moss st 5, work 16th row of chart to end.

Work a further 24 rows as set.

Next row Patt to last 5 sts, cast off these 5 sts.

Leave rem 61 sts on a spare needle.

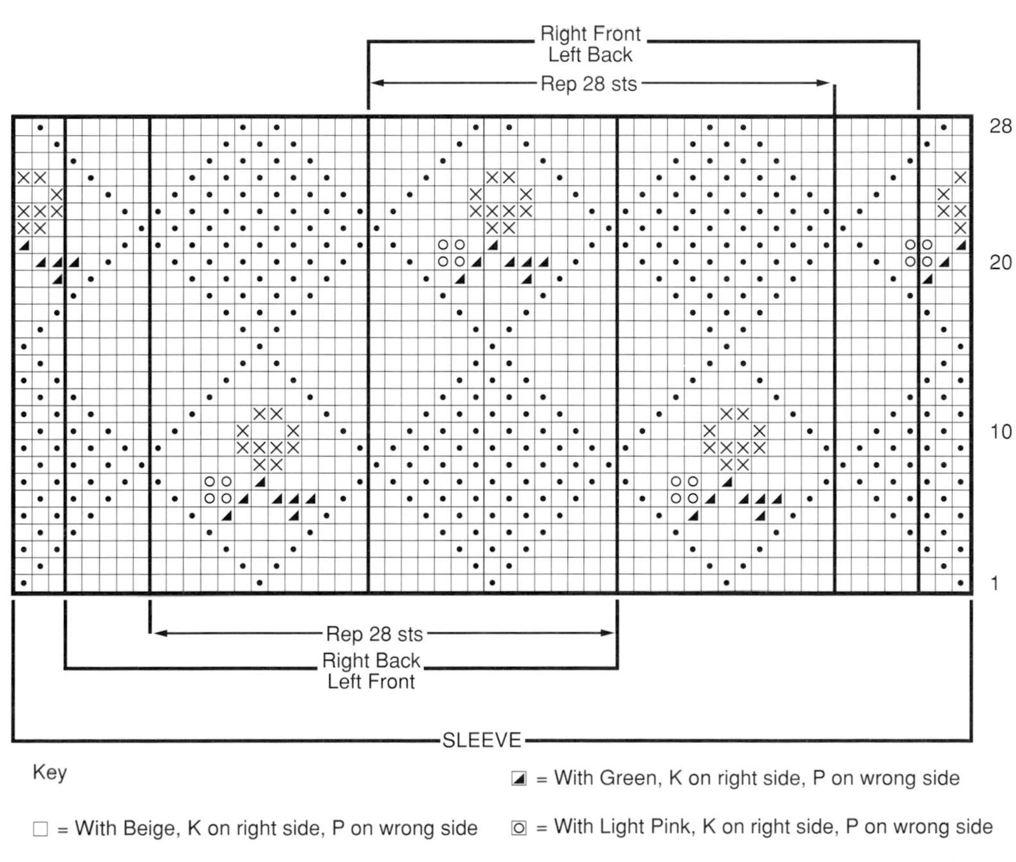

Key

□ = With Beige, K on right side, P on wrong side

⊡ = With Beige, P on right side, K on wrong side

◢ = With Green, K on right side, P on wrong side

◎ = With Light Pink, K on right side, P on wrong side

⊠ = With Dark Pink, K on right side, P on wrong side

LEFT BACK
With 3mm (No 11/US 2) needles and A, cast on 66 sts.
1st row (right side) [P1, k1] to end.
2nd row [K1, p1] to end.
These 2 rows form moss st. Moss st 6 rows more.
Change to 3¼mm (No 10/US 3) needles.
1st row With A, moss st 5, work 15th row of chart to end.
2nd row Work 16th row of chart to last 5 sts, with A, moss st 5.
Work a further 25 rows as set.
Back
Next row Patt to end then patt across sts of Right Back. 127 sts.
Cont in patt across all sts, dec one st at each end of next row and 6 foll 6th rows. 113 sts. Work 4cm/1½in straight, ending with a wrong side row.
Inc one st at each end of next row and 6 foll 4th rows, working inc sts into patt. 127 sts. Cont straight until Back measures 37cm/14½in from beg, ending with a wrong side row.
Shape Armholes
Cast off 8 sts at beg of next 2 rows.
Dec one st at each end of next 5 rows. 101 sts. Cont straight until Back measures 59cm/23¼in from beg, ending with a wrong side row.
Shape Shoulders
Cast off 10 sts at beg of next 4 rows and 9 sts at beg of foll 2 rows. Cast off rem 43 sts.

LEFT FRONT
With 3mm (No 11/US 2) needles and A, cast on 66 sts.
Work 8 rows in moss st as given for Right Back.
Change to 3¼mm (No 10/US 3) needles.
1st row Work 1st row of chart to last 5 sts, with A, moss st 5.
2nd row With A, moss st 5, work 2nd row of chart to end.
Work a further 26 rows as set.
Cont in patt, dec one st at side edge on next row and 6 foll 6th rows. 59 sts.
Work 4cm/1½in straight, ending with a wrong side row.
Inc one st at side edge on next row and 6 foll 4th rows. 66 sts. Cont straight until Front matches Back to armhole shaping, ending at side edge.
Shape Armhole
Cast off 8 sts at beg of next row. Work 1 row. Dec one st at armhole edge on next 5 rows. 53 sts. Patt 1 row straight.
Shape Neck
Next row Patt to last 5 sts, turn; leave the 5 sts on a safety pin.
Dec one st at neck edge only on next row and every foll 3rd row until 29 sts rem. Cont straight until Front matches Back to shoulder shaping, ending at armhole edge.
Shape Shoulder
Cast off 10 sts at beg of next row and foll alt row. Work 1 row. Cast off.
Mark front band to indicate position of 5 buttons: first one 11cm/4¼in from lower edge, last one 2cm/¾in below neck shaping and rem 3 evenly spaced between.

RIGHT FRONT
With 3mm (No 11/US 2) needles and A, cast on 66 sts.
Work 8 rows in moss st as given for Left Back.
Change to 3¼mm (No 10/US 3) needles.
1st row With A, moss st 5, work 1st row of chart to end.
2nd row Work 2nd row of chart to last 5 sts, with A, moss st 5.
Complete as Left Front, making buttonholes to markers as follows:
Buttonhole row (right side) Moss st 1, k2 tog, yf, moss st 2, patt to end.

SLEEVES
With 3mm (No 11/US 2) needles and A, cast on 57 sts.
1st row P1, [k1, p1] to end.
This row forms moss st. Moss st 9 rows more.
Change to 3¼mm (No 10/US 3) needles.
Work in patt from chart, inc one st at each end of 3rd row and every foll 6th row until there are 101 sts, working inc sts into patt. Cont straight until Sleeve measures 45cm/17¾in from beg, ending with a wrong side row. Mark each end of last row.
Shape Top
Work a further 8 rows. Dec one st at each end of next row and 3 foll alt rows. 93 sts. Patt 1 row. Cast off.

COLLAR
With 3mm (No 11/US 2) needles, rejoin A yarn at inside edge to 5 sts on right front safety pin. Cont in moss st, inc one st at inside edge on 3rd row and every foll 4th row until there are 20 sts. Work straight until Collar, when slightly stretched, fits along shaped edge of front to centre of back neck. Leave these sts on a spare needle.
Work other half of collar to match.
With right sides of collar pieces together, cast off together collar sts (see diagrams page 18).

TO MAKE UP
Join shoulder seams. Sew collar in place. Sew in sleeves, sewing rows above markers to cast off sts at armholes. Beginning above welt, join side seams, then sleeve seams. Sew on buttons. Place the 5 cast off sts of right back under the first 5 sts of left back and slip stitch in place.

Bobble and cable tunic

This longline textured tunic has a cable and bobble stitch pattern, and is knitted in a four-ply cotton. It has a garter stitch shawl collar which is softened by a pretty picot edge.

MATERIALS

22 50g balls of Rowan Cotton Glace.
Pair each of 3¼mm (No 10/US 3) and 3¾mm (No 9/US 4) knitting needles.
One 3¼mm (No 10/US 3) circular needle.
Cable needle.

MEASUREMENTS

To fit bust	81-91 cm 32-36 in
Actual bust measurement	114 cm 45 in
Length	73 cm 28¾ in
Sleeve seam	44 cm 17¼ in

TENSION

28.5 sts and 35 rows to 10cm/4in square over pattern on 3¾mm (No 9/US 4) needles.

ABBREVIATIONS

C4B = sl next 2 sts onto cable needle and leave at back of work, k2, then k2 from cable needle;
C4F = sl next 2 sts onto cable needle and leave at front of work, k2, then k2 from cable needle;
Cr3L = sl next 2 sts onto cable needle and leave at front of work, p1, then k2 from cable needle;
Cr3R = sl next st onto cable needle and leave at back of work, k2, then p1 from cable needle;
mb = pick up loop lying between st just worked and next st, work into front, back, front, back and front of the loop, then pass 2nd, 3rd, 4th and 5th sts over 1st st.

Also see page 7.

BACK

With 3¼mm (No 10/US 3) needles cast on 162 sts.
1st rib row (right side) [P2, k2] twice, *p1, k4, p1, [k2, p2] 3 times, k2; rep from * to last 14 sts, p1, k4, p1, [k2, p2] twice.
2nd rib row [K2, p2] twice, *k1, p4, k1, [p2, k2] 3 times, p2; rep from * to last 14 sts, k1, p4, k1, [p2, k2] twice.
3rd rib row [P2, k2] twice, *p1, C4B, p1, k2, p2, k2, p1, mb, p1, then pass bobble st over the p st, k2, p2, k2; rep from * to last 14 sts, p1, C4B, p1, [k2, p2] twice.
4th rib row As 2nd row.
These 4 rows form rib. Rib a further 14 rows.
Change to 3¾mm (No 9/US 4) needles.
1st row P9, [C4B, p8, mb, p1, then pass bobble st over the p st, p7] to last 13 sts, C4B, p9.
2nd row K9, [p4, k16] to last 13 sts, p4, k9.
3rd row P7, [C4B, C4F, p12] to last 15 sts, C4B, C4F, p7.
4th row K7, [p8, k12] to last 15 sts, p8, k7.
5th row P5, [C4B, k4, C4F, p4, mb, p1, then pass bobble st over the p st, p3] to last 17 sts, C4B, k4, C4F, p5.
6th row K5, [p2, k2, p4, k2, p2, k8] to last 17 sts, p2, k2, p4, k2, p2, k5.
7th row P3, *[C4B, k2] twice, C4F, p4; rep from * to last 19 sts, [C4B, k2] twice, C4F, p3.
8th row K3, [p2, k4, p4, k4, p2, k4] to last 19 sts, p2, k4, p4, k4, p2, k3.
9th row P1, [C4B, k12, C4F] to last st, p1.
10th row K1, [p2, k6, p4, k6, p2] to last st, k1.
11th row P1, [Cr3L, k5, C4B, k5, Cr3R] to last st, p1.
12th row K2, [p2, k5, p4, k5, p2, k2] to end.
13th row P2, [Cr3L, k12, Cr3R, p2] to end.
14th row As 8th row.
15th row P3, [Cr3L, k3, C4B, k3, Cr3R, p2, mb, p1, pass bobble st over the p st, p1] to last 19 sts, Cr3L, k3, C4B, k3, Cr3R, p3.
16th row K4, [p2, k3, p4, k3, p2, k6] to last 18 sts, p2, k3, p4, k3, p2, k4.
17th row P4, [Cr3L, k8, Cr3R, p6] to last 18 sts, Cr3L, k8, Cr3R, p4.
18th row As 6th row.

19th row P5, [Cr3L, k1, C4B, k1, Cr3R, p4, mb, p1, then pass bobble st over the p st, p3] to last 17 sts, Cr3L, k1, C4B, k1, Cr3R, p5.
20th row K6, [p2, k1, p4, k1, p2, k10] to last 16 sts, p2, k1, p4, k1, p2, k6.
21st row P6, [Cr3L, k4, Cr3R, p10] to last 16 sts, Cr3L, k4, Cr3R, p6.
22nd row As 4th row.
23rd row P7, [Cr3L, k2, Cr3R, p6, mb, p1, then pass bobble st over the p st, p5] to last 15 sts, Cr3L, k2, Cr3R, p7.
24th row K8, [p6, k14] to last 14 sts, p6, k8.
25th row P8, [Cr3L, Cr3R, p14] to last 14 sts, Cr3L, Cr3R, p8.
26th row As 2nd row.
These 26 rows form patt. Cont in patt until Back measures 73cm/28¾in from beg, ending with a wrong side row.

Shape Shoulders
Cast off 19 sts at beg of next 4 rows and 20 sts at beg of foll 2 rows. Cast off rem 46 sts.

FRONT

Work as given for Back until Front measures 50cm/19¾in from beg, ending with a right side row.

Shape Neck
Next row Patt 69, cast off next 24 sts, patt to end.
Cont on last set of sts only. Dec one st at neck edge on 5th row and every foll 6th row until 58 sts rem. Cont straight until Front matches Back to shoulder shaping, ending at side edge.

Shape Shoulder
Cast off 19 sts at beg of next row and foll alt row. Work 1 row. Cast off rem 20 sts.
With right side facing, rejoin yarn to rem sts and complete as first side.

SLEEVES

With 3¼mm (No 10/US 3) needles cast on 62 sts.
Work 18 rows in rib as given for Back.
Change to 3¾mm (No 9/US 4) needles.
Work in patt as given for Back, inc one st at each end of every 3rd row until there are 92 sts then on every foll 4th row until there are 130 sts, working inc sts into patt. Cont straight until Sleeve measures 44cm/17¼in from beg, ending with a wrong side row.
Cast off.

COLLAR

Join shoulder seams.
With 3¼mm (No 10/US 3) circular needle and right side facing, k up 60 sts up right front neck, 36 sts across back neck and 60 sts down left front neck. 156 sts. Work backwards and forwards in rows. K 1 row.
Next 2 rows K to last 54 sts, turn.
Next 2 rows K to last 48 sts, turn.
Next 2 rows K to last 42 sts, turn.
Cont in this way, working 6 sts more at end of every row, work 12 rows. K 39 rows across all sts.
Dec row K6, [k2 tog, k11] to last 7 sts, k2 tog, k5. 144 sts.
Next row Cast off knitwise 2 sts, [sl st used in casting off back onto left hand needle, cast on 2 sts knitwise, cast off 4 sts knitwise] to end.
Fasten off.

TO MAKE UP

Sew on sleeves, placing centre of sleeves to shoulder seams. Join side and sleeve seams. Lap right side of collar over left side and catch down row ends of collar together to cast off sts at centre of front.